ADVANCE REVIEWS OF *THE PRISONER AND THE PENGUIN*

"The Prisoner is Terry Waite. The Penguin is the brand that markets the books. The Penguin engineers the value of the books through quality, attention to detail, commitment indeed to The Prisoner (ie, the consumer). Giles Lury in his latest book has written this and 75 other very short (marketing) stories. They will go viral" – Professor Scott Lash, Director, Centre for Cultural Studies, Goldsmiths, University of London.

"An Aesop for marketers. Goes to show that every brand should have at least one great story to tell" – Paul Sweeney, Head of Brand, Paddy Power.

"A great book. It goes to show that the best brands are often built on simple but honest values" – Nick Jenkins, Founder, Moonpig.

"Giles is truly the bard of brands. His business insight shines through in this new collection of marketing maxims as does his passion to pass on the accumulated wisdom of a life steeped in brands and branding" – Tim Kaner, Director of Marketing and Communications, University of Bath.

"The wonderful thing about Giles' brand stories is that it doesn't matter whether or not they are true, altered, exaggerated or amended – what makes them so powerful is the intrigue and surprise. On reading the 'stories' I felt I was being educated about the true meaning of brands and entertained at the same time" – Katy Mousinho, Head of Insight & Customer Experience, Thomas Cook.

"Giles' new book is a superb collection of marketing tales that will educate, inspire, entertain and help you live with your brand happily ever after" – Paul Walton, CEO & Founder, Strategic Leaps.

"A consummate feat of edutainment. Every marketer should read and enjoy this book" – Mark Scott, CEO, Cello Group.

"The moral of every story is immediately applicable. A good read with valuable lessons" – Christopher Satterthwaite, CEO, Chime Communications plc.

Published by
LID Publishing Ltd.
The Loft, 19a Floral Street
London WC2E 9DS (United Kingdom)
info@lidpublishing.com
LIDpublishing.com

A member of:

www.businesspublishersroundtable.com

Printed by CPI Group (UK) Ltd, Croydon, CR0 4YY

ISBN: 978-1-907794-51-3

Design: e-Digital Design Ltd
All illustrations by Dawn Childs

The Prisoner and the Penguin

and 75 other modern marketing stories

Giles Lury

THE VALUE ENGINEERS

For Karen...

INTRODUCTION

I want to tell you a story...

This book aims to be an alternative to traditional marketing handbooks. Rather than a textbook, it is first and foremost meant to be an enjoyable "storybook" to which the reader can dip into. They can read short tales about some of the world's leading brands: their origins, their actions, their innovations, their beliefs and in some cases their demise.

However, like many good storybooks, it's more than just stories: it was written to communicate a message. In this case, it aims to help businesspeople – from general managers to marketing managers to aspiring marketers – think about and understand more of the principles of good branding.

To this end, all of the stories have a "moral", highlighting a principle or a lesson from which other brands can learn.

The power of a good story

This book is far from being the first to recognize the power of a good story. Scheherazade managed to keep herself alive for 1,001 nights by leaving her stories unfinished overnight, keeping her husband, the young sultan, in suspense. Troubadours and minstrels earned their living telling stories and singing for their suppers. Novels, movies, comics and, some might say, parts of the press are all modern forms of storytelling. It seems that, as a race, we humans love a good story.

Stories aren't just for enjoyment, though, they have long been a powerful tool for teaching; the interesting expression of the particular to make or illustrate a more general point.

Jesus used parables as the basis for His teaching. *The Karma Sutra* may have a role as a manual for sexual techniques but it was originally the story of a young maiden in India. The Victorians loved their rhyming *Cautionary Tales*. Aesop told his fables.

The Archers, the BBC radio series that has run for over 13,000 episodes, was originally intended as a drama-based educational programme. The Government hoped farmers would listen to the stories but simultaneously pick up messages that would help them feed a still-rationed Britain.

Once upon a brand

Today's companies are increasingly recognizing that one of the best ways to help ensure a prosperous future for their brands is to tell stories about themselves and their brands. Not only does this ensure all of their employees know and understand their history but it helps teach them about the values and the behaviours that they wish to encourage. Compared to PowerPoint presentations and traditional training sessions, stories are more engaging, better remembered and provide the heroes, the "role models", that employees can aspire to or follow.

Nike has a number of Ekins (Nike backwards), senior executives who spend much of their time serving as "corporate storytellers". They tell the company's stories to everyone from vice presidents to sales reps to the hourly workers who run the cash registers at Nike's stores. Nelson Farris, Nike's Director of Corporate Education and the company's chief Ekin, is on record as saying: "Our stories are not about extraordinary business plans or financial manipulations; they're about people getting things done."

One of the stories an Ekin might tell is how legendary track and field coach and Nike co-founder Bill Bowerman, who on deciding that his team needed better running shoes went out to his workshop and poured rubber into the family waffle iron. The real power of this story is that it is not just an engaging tale of how Nike's famous "waffle sole" was born, but also a demonstration of Nike's spirit of innovation.

The stories spread

As such stories are told and retold, their impact spreads, reaching far beyond a specific company's employees. The stories are told to, heard by and retold by two other groups of people.

The general public – you and I – are hearing these stories more and more frequently. We find them on the Internet, on TV, in the newspaper or on the radio. They are becoming part of the social currency around brands and often have a very positive effect on the overall perceptions of the brand in question.

One example is the Nordstrom story to be found on page 104 – A tired old story? Not only does it teach Nordstrom employees what the brand's values are and what behaviours are expected of them, but when customers and non-customers hear it, they learn about a retailer that takes real pride in its customer service.

Because of their power of influence, some brands are explicitly using their stories both internally and externally. For brands like Apple, Nike, Virgin, Coke and innocent, stories are integral to their PR strategies. Coke uses digital storytelling at its Coca-Cola World Centre in Atlanta, from which the Iris Bell story, Daddy's good luck charm, comes (page 76).

Admittedly, stories aren't always positive. Some stories can be damaging: Nike's The stitching and the e-mail is a classic example. A story that Nike must wish had never become so public but which is on page 60.

The second group of people who are now hearing and retelling stories is made up of business leaders and marketers, who are hearing and reading stories about other brands and even their competitors. For this audience, such stories can play two roles. The "morals" of these stories can offer lessons about what they might want to do – or not do – with their brands and in their marketing. The stories also raise the inevitable question: "Shouldn't we have stories to tell about our brand?"; starting their hearers on a search to identify anecdotes about their own histories.

This book hopes to play a role in the spreading of this new breed of brand stories beyond their internal audiences, and to provide inspiration and lessons for business and brand mangers everywhere.

A few are more general stories which talk about specific aspects of branding, insight and innovation. The title story – The prisoner and the penguin on page 15 – is not just a heart-warming story but also a demonstration of the power of good branding and the role that visual icons can play.

In search of a good story

The specific stories in the book have been collected and selected by me over a number of years. Some I know from first-hand experience or from having worked on the brand, some come from talking to people who were involved. Others come from research and hearsay, but I have tried to give credit to the books, newspapers, magazines, websites and people who provided them.

To the best of my knowledge they are "true", but some may have been altered, exaggerated or amended with their telling and retelling, so I hope anyone who knows better will forgive any liberties they feel may have been inadvertently taken.

Finally, with this book as proof, I believe the real power of stories is in their telling and re-telling. They may grow and change but the best live on and on. They are enjoyable and can be educational, so I hope you enjoy reading the ones here but I also hope you enjoy re-telling these stories.

Finally, if you know a great brand story that isn't included then please do send it to me at giles.lury@thevalueengineers.com because I love hearing a new story even more than I like telling an old one.

The other characters in the story of this book

The story of this book is a long one and there are many characters that have played an important part in its writing and to whom I owe my thanks:

The friends, family, colleagues and clients who have shared their stories.

Lou Ellerton, who helped in so many ways, from encouraging me to keep going, for suggestions and ideas, for editing and proof reading (of which I needed lots!).

Dawn Childs, who designed and redesigned the cover for me and who created the illustrations which help add the character I wanted for the final book.

My fellow Directors at The Value Engineers, who have supported and encouraged me along the way.

To Adam, my brother, for timely support, suggestions and for first telling me the story of The prisoner and the penguin.

And of course to my wife and family, who have put up with my scribbling.

Giles Lury

The Value Engineers

IT'S STORY TIME

1 THE PRISONER AND THE PENGUIN

In 1987, Terry Waite, the then Archbishop of Canterbury's Special Envoy to the Middle East, was kidnapped. It made headline news around the world and was the beginning of what was to be a four-year period of captivity for the man from Cheshire, UK.

Slowly but surely, Terry Waite started to win the respect of his guards. Due to the language barriers, however, conversations were limited.

So, when after many months one of the guards offered to try and get Terry Waite a book, he had to think carefully about what to ask for. Would the guard understand what he wanted if he requested a particular book, and what was the likelihood of finding that specific book anyway?

Finally, after much thought, he decided what he would ask for: he asked the guard for any book which had a picture of a particular bird on the spine. To ensure the guard knew what he meant, he drew him a picture of the black and white bird he was referring to: a penguin.

Asked later to explain his thinking, Terry Waite said that he felt anything published by Penguin would be a good book and worth reading.

And the moral is that a recognizable brand icon is a powerful communication equity. What communication equities does your brand own?

2 THE TATTOOED ANKLE

Phil Knight and Bill Bowerman met at the University of Oregon. Phil Knight was a student and Bill Bowerman was the athletics coach whose dedication led him to make running shoes by hand for his star pupils. In 1957 they founded Blue Ribbon Sports and began selling high-tech, low-priced shoes out of the back of a van in California.

In 1972, the company was renamed after the Greek goddess of victory and adopted a new logo designed for the company by a student for the princely sum of $25. Nike and the famous red swoosh are now instantly recognizable all over the world.

Like most rags to riches stories, however, there have been downs as well as ups. Most notably the bad publicity surrounding claims about the poor working conditions of Asian workers producing shoes in China, Indonesia, Thailand and Vietnam, for which Phil Knight publicly apologized. Other "downs" have included plateau-ing sales of trainers, increased competition from old stagers like Adidas, and claims that Nike put undue pressure on Brazilian coach Mario Zagello to play an unfit Ronaldo in the 1998 World Cup Final against France.

That Nike has come through these is in no small part down to its key employees. The designers are recruited from a range of backgrounds, not just from art schools. Employees come from transportation design schools, architectural design and even occasionally NASA. They are well looked after at Nike's headquarters in Beaverton, Oregon. It's a 75-acre site that's home to sports centres, gyms, design studios and marketing suites as well as various lakes, small woods, restaurants, cafes and a day-care centre for employees' children.

Above all these, Nike's greatest asset is the fanatical loyalty it engenders amongst its employees. A few years ago, a sceptical journalist for *The Sunday Times* was being shown around the headquarters. He asked about the apocryphal stories of dedicated workers having the red swoosh tattooed on their bodies. The man conducting the tour was Nelson Farris, the Corporate Education Director, who promptly rolled up his trouser leg and said: "You mean like this?"

And the moral is that great brands inspire great loyalty. How will your brand inspire this level of loyalty?

3 FROM SWITZERLAND WITH LOVE

In the early 1950s, Ruth Handler was watching her daughter, Barbara, play with paper dolls, and noticed that she gave them adult roles. This was unexpected, as at the time, most children's toy dolls were representations of babies or young children. Taken with her observation, Ruth suggested the idea of an adult-bodied doll to her husband, Elliot, who just happened to be a senior executive at the Mattel toy company. He was unenthusiastic about the idea, as were Mattel's directors.

And nothing happened until after the Handler's summer vacation to Switzerland in 1956, where Ruth noticed a strange looking doll in the window of a cigarette shop. The doll was 11 and a half inches tall, had platinum-blond hair, long legs and perhaps surprisingly an ample bosom. Her name was Bild Lilli.[1]

Although Ruth didn't know it at the time – she didn't speak German – the doll was actually a sex symbol, sold mainly to middle-aged men. (That's why the doll was only stocked in bars and tobacco stores.) Instead, she took one look at the blond Bild Lilli and saw a perfect toy for young girls. She bought three of them. She gave one to her daughter and took the others back to Mattel.

The design of the doll was slightly reworked (with help from engineer Jack Ryan) and the doll was given a new name, Barbie, after Handler's daughter, Barbara. The doll made its debut at the American International Toy Fair in New York on 9 March 1959. (This date is now used as Barbie's official birthday.)

While Barbie wasn't exactly an overnight success – early market research showed that some parents were unhappy

1 And just in case you're interested, The Bild Lilli doll was based on a character that appeared in a comic strip drawn by Reinhard Beuthin for the newspaper *Die Bild-Zeitung*. Lilli was a blonde bombshell, a working girl who knew what she wanted and was not above using men to get it. The Lilli doll was first sold in Germany in 1955. Mattel acquired the rights to the Bild Lilli doll in 1964 and production of Lilli was stopped.

about the doll's chest, and the famous US Sears store initially refused to carry a toy that had "feminine curves" – around 350,000 Barbie dolls were sold during the first year of production. Since then the toy has become a cultural icon and one of the most popular toys in the world.

And the moral is that old ideas can be reinterpreted for new markets. What ideas from other markets could you use to deliver innovation in your own market?

4 THE MOUSE AND THE CAR PARK ATTENDANT

Walt Disney created Mickey Mouse but it was his wife who actually christened him. Walt went on to create: "A place for people to find happiness and knowledge". On 23 September 1955, the 30th wedding anniversary of Walt and Lillian Disney, Disneyland California opened its doors.

This wonderful world succeeds without any consumers; it doesn't even have any customers. It has succeeded without employees. It has no staff.

This land only has "guests" and they are served by "cast members", each performing their own role.

But it isn't this special Hollywood-style labelling of visitors and workers that makes Disney the huge success it is. Rather, it is the attention to detail that was instilled in it by its creator and that has been maintained ever since. It is a company that believes each and every cast member is crucial in ensuring that guests have a truly unforgettable, magical experience.

In an interview, Michael Eisner, then Chief Executive Officer, stressed the importance, not of the mouse and the cast member who portrays him, but the role of the car park attendants. Where others might view these attendants as having junior, unimportant and uncreative roles, Eisner said:

"They are the first people our guests usually meet when they arrive, so they are probably our most important cast members. They have to be ready to answer questions on everything that may be happening that day in the parks, such as times of the parades or the good value places to eat lunch."

And the moral is that everyone in service brands is in marketing. Are your employees delivering your brand in their interactions with the public?

5 THE SAMPLE OF ONE

Market research is a valuable tool in marketing. It provides decision-makers with information and guidance on the decisions and choices they need to make.

Sometimes someone is just so sure that they have a winning idea they just act on it.

Richard Branson is one such man.

Interviewed for the book *The Company Man*, he said that all the insight he needed to create Virgin Atlantic was one phone call, or rather the lack of one:

"I decided that there must be room for another airline after I spent two days trying to get through to People's Express. That was the sum of my market research."

And the moral is that sometimes you don't need great swathes of market research. Is all your market research really necessary?

6 THE CHOCOLATE LOVER TAKEN FOR A FOOL

Some stories are best told by those who are leading characters in their own tales. James Averdieck tells the story of how he was tricked into choosing the name for his new chocolate lovers' brand...

"I'm entrepreneurial and always have been. And I've always been a chocolate-lover. In terms of the business, my best decision was going with the Gü brand name. I worked with a marketing agency right from the start, and asked them to come up with a brand name for us, because they're impossible to come up with.

"I'd been down that route before, and it can be a futile exercise. They phoned me a week later, and told me that they'd been round lots of chocolate shops in Europe and had come across a brand called Gü. The name was exactly what I wanted, but

I'd never seen that brand before.

"They showed me the packet and I was really disappointed that someone had beaten me to it. It was then that they told me it was a fake – they'd mocked it up for me – and that was the brand name I should go with. I like Gü because it reminds you of gooey chocolate, and the umlaut adds a Continental sophistication."

(James Averdieck interviewed in *Management Today*, 8 January 2005.)

And the moral is that brand naming is never easy. Do you know what you want from any new brand names?

7 BEAUTY AND THE TWO UNDERTAKERS

In 1976, Gordon Roddick left for an expedition which was to take him from Buenos Aires to New York on horseback. He left behind his young wife, Anita. Anita needed some means of supporting herself and their young family while he was away and after considering a number of options she decided that she wanted to open a shop selling cosmetics.

This was to be no ordinary cosmetics shop; she wanted to follow the practice of Tahitian women who made cosmetics using local, natural products. She wanted to eschew the traditional glossy, highly packaged, highly advertised approach of many beauty firms.

She wanted to champion recycling, natural products and a fair return for the producers of the all-important ingredients.

The store still needed a name. Whilst travelling in America, Anita had seen a car bodywork garage named "The Body Shop". She had immediately liked the name and now she remembered it. A student created a logo for her for the princely sum of £25.

Her choice of name, however, wasn't popular with two undertakers who had premises close to her first store in Brighton. They thought the name might be bad for their trade and she received a letter from their solicitors. Rather than give up on her new brand name, Anita decided to fight for it. She contacted the local paper and told them her story. They reprinted it in a double-page spread providing wonderful free publicity just in time for the store's launch.

On Saturday 27 March 1976, The Body Shop opened its doors to the public for the first time. The day's takings were £130. Fast-forward 27 years, and The Body Shop now has more than 1,500 stores worldwide.

The brand still doesn't use traditional advertising, although it exploits all the opportunities it gets to promote itself using its store windows, in-store posters and leaflets, lorries and any PR opportunities that arise.

Anita Roddick has appeared in a commercial, however. It was part of a campaign for American Express where celebrities talked about how American Express helped them to conduct their business. Anita had stuck to her principles of not spending her money advertising The

Body Shop but had found another means of gaining free publicity for her brand.

And the moral is that PR is not only one of the most powerful media for a brand, but it's also free. What is it about your brand that would make a PR story?

8 THE CHARM BRACELET AND THE 52 FUNDAMENTAL ERRORS

So what can you make from an oil cloth, some free paint samples, some beading picked up at a timber yard, some old cardboard and the charms from your wife's bracelet?

If you were Charles Darrow, you'd create a pastime that your family would know simply as "The Game".

Now better known as Monopoly, The Game was created by Darrow when he was an unemployed equipment salesman in 1929. The oil-cloth formed his board, coloured and decorated with the paint samples. The beading was cut into pieces and became the original houses and hotels. The charms from his wife's bracelet were the tokens. The street names were the real street names of Atlantic City, where in better times Darrow had liked to spend his summer with his family.

Word about The Game started to spread, and Darrow was soon making first two, then six sets a day. When in 1934 Darrow received his first order from a department store, Wannamaker in Philadelphia, he decided it might be time to expand.

He approached established games company Parker Brothers, but it rejected it, saying that it had: "52 fundamental errors". Darrow ignored its comments and went on making Monopoly. Sales continued to grow and some 20,000 sets were produced in 1934.

When news of his continued success reached Parker Brothers, the company decided it had been a little hasty in its initial assessment. It offered Darrow a deal that included an attractive royalty for every set sold.

Darrow retired at 46 and died a millionaire aged 78. While it is not confirmed, it's widely believed he bought his wife another charm bracelet with some of his royalties.

And the moral is that don't be too proud to admit your mistakes. How can you change a past mistake into a future opportunity?

9 TO DYE FOR

(This story is adapted from Dave Trott's blog)

Shirley Polykoff was a copywriter in the era now made famous by the TV series *Mad Men*.

One of her early accounts was Clairol, a brand that at the time faced a number of challenges. Perhaps its biggest issue was that, having your hair dyed blonde in the 1950s marked you out as a good-time girl. It suggested that you slept around.

This made Shirley Polykoff angry. She felt a woman should be entitled to do whatever she wanted with her body.

Out of that anger arose the now famous Clairol ad campaign. Shirley's aim was to turn around the image of blondes. She proposed using Doris Day, "girl-next-door" blondes in the advertising, alongside the headline, "Does she, or doesn't she?". The sub-head would read: "Colour so natural only her hairdresser knows for sure".

As Dave Trott, no mean (m)adman himself, said: "The brilliance was using that headline against those models – with a picture of a fresh, wholesome blonde, the answer wasn't so obvious." The girls looked too innocent to be sleeping around.

It was a very difficult campaign to sell and even harder for the client to buy. Many at the agency tried to kill it, and the clients weren't sure it was the right image for Clairol.

So while everyone finally agreed to run the campaign, they were equally ready to pull it at the first sign of trouble. All of that changed when letters started coming into Clairol.

One particular letter stood out. It said:

"Thank you for changing my life. My boyfriend Harold and I

were keeping company for five years but he never wanted to set a date. This made me very nervous. I am 28 and my mother kept saying soon it would be too late for me. Then, I saw a Clairol ad in the subway. I decided to take a chance and dyed my hair blonde, and that is how I am in Bermuda now on my honeymoon with Harold."

Everyone loved that letter. It was circulated around the entire company and used as the theme for a national sales meeting. The doubts about the campaign disappeared.

Over the next decade, the percentage of women colouring their hair rose from 7% to 40% and the image of blondes moved from being brassy to being fresh, confident and fun. The market grew from $25 million a year to $200 million, and Clairol took half of it.

But what made Shirley Polykoff a real genius in Dave Trott's eyes wasn't having the idea for the campaign but something that came to light many years later. At the leaving party for her retirement in 1973, a number of speeches talked about how her campaign had helped pave the way for women's equality and feminism. Shirley Polykoff stood up, thanked everyone and asked if they remembered the particular letter that had given everyone the courage to get behind the campaign. Of course everyone smiled and nodded.

Shirley Polykoff said: *"Actually, I wrote that letter."*

And the moral is that sometimes, creating a truly powerful brand or campaign means changing the way people think. Should your brand challenge a convention?

10 THE INSPIRATIONAL BIRTHDAY CAKE

Walls started producing ice-cream in 1922. In the intervening years, it has become one of the world's best-known brands, always seeking to grow and develop new ideas. While it has introduced hundreds of innovations in its time, perhaps the strangest source of any was that of a birthday cake.

In 1980, one of the Walls' new product development team received a special birthday cake. His wife had come across a recipe for *"mille-feuille"*, the French confection made from layers of puff pastry and cream. Translated, the name means *"a thousand leaves"*.

After a splendid birthday supper, she revealed her surprise – the mille-feuille. The reaction was all she could have hoped for. He loved the unique textural combination of thin, crispy pastry and rich, smooth, thick cream.

The next day at work, he was telling a colleague what a wonderful birthday cake his wife had made him, when inspiration struck. What if he recreated the delicious eating experience of a mille-feuille in the form of an ice-cream?

Ice-cream was a natural alternative to cream and after only a little thought, it was agreed that very thin layers of chocolate seemed a mouth-watering alternative to the pastry.

Like many other innovations, while the idea seemed simple, the execution was far from it. New processes for layering ice-cream and spraying ultra-thin layers of chocolate had to be developed, piloted and finally put into practice.

At last everything was in place and the first Walls Viennettas were produced, distributed and sold. Today, Viennetta is still a top-selling ice-cream in over 50 countries.

And the moral is that inspiration for innovation can come from adjacent markets. Where are you looking for your next innovation?

11 THE MANAGEMENT WHO FIRED THEMSELVES

One day in 1985, Andrew Grove invited his Chairman into his office and suggested they fire themselves.

Neither had been embezzling company funds; there was no sex scandal. It wasn't even as if they had been doing a bad job, but their brand, Intel, was increasingly struggling to match the price/value offer of its Japanese competitors in its primary market of memory chips. It was getting harder and harder to make any profit while still remaining price competitive.

Grove felt that there was a need to take a completely fresh perspective on the company. He wanted to review all the everyday assumptions that tended to dictate the way Intel operated. The assumptions that had been in place for so long that they were accepted almost as if they were the rules of doing business.

He suggested to Gordon Moore, his Chairman, that they physically walk down and out of the building as if they had actually been fired. Once outside, they would turn around and re-enter the building; not as the current management team who were doing a *"good enough"* job, but as a hot-shot replacement management team who were going to turn the brand around.

Sitting down again after their short but mind-clearing walk, they looked at the existing plans and set themselves the objective of not just doing them all over again, but doing them better this time. They went through the plans and the assumptions behind them. Everything was up for review.

The result? They decided that one of their most fundamental assumptions was wrong. They were in the wrong business. Grove and Moore decided to shift the focus of the business and the brand away from memory chips to what, until then, had been a secondary priority. In the future, Intel would focus on microprocessors.

And the moral is that "good enough" is not enough. What are you planning to do that is ground-breaking, not just good enough?

12 WHEN 250,000 PEOPLE WERE WRONG

According to some surveys, Coca-Cola is the second most recognized word in the world (after "OK"). It's certainly regarded by most in the marketing industry as one of the world's most valuable brands.

It's strange to think that as the 1980s dawned, Coca-Cola was facing the frightening prospect of losing its number one spot in the American soft drinks market.

Pepsi's aggressive "Take the Taste Challenge" campaign was winning it market share, leaving Coke relying ever more for its market leading position on its dominance in restricted markets such as vending machines and fast-food outlets.

The success of the brand's stable mate, Diet Coke, was adding to the problem. As sales of Diet Coke rose and people converted to the new brand, the pool of available sugar cola drinkers was decreasing.

The team in Atlanta embarked on a mission to beat the Pepsi challenge. Blind taste tests were conducted, in which US consumers were given unbranded samples to drink and rate. The tests showed that people preferred the taste of Pepsi to that of Coke.

On the basis of the research, the team at Coca-Cola decided to develop a new recipe for their flagship brand. The new formulation was based on Diet Coke, but used high fructose corn syrup to create a drink that was sweeter, smoother and a bit more like Pepsi.

Word has it that Coke then undertook the largest ever programme of taste-testing research, interviewing over a quarter of a million people. A clear and significant majority of these preferred the taste of New Coke.

So what should the executives in Atlanta do: launch New Coke alongside "Old" Coke or replace it outright? Worried that retaining both recipes would split sales, giving market leadership to Pepsi, the team chose to replace the old formula with New Coke. The need to maintain secrecy, however, meant that consumers were never asked for their views; a mistake that would come back to haunt the business.

On 23 April 1985 New Coke was launched, and production of the original formulation halted later that week. America was outraged – so much so that by 11 July senior executives were forced to hold a press conference to announce the return of Classic Coke.

Rather than welcoming the "better tasting" New Coke, millions of Americans decided they hated it before they tried it. Despite a recipe that was preferred in blind taste-tests, the vast majority of those who did taste it convinced themselves they still preferred the original!

To its consumers, Coke was much more than just a product. It was an institution; a way of life. It was something they had grown up with; something with which they felt they had a relationship. It was their brand. They reacted with horror. They protested long and loud.

Luckily for Coke, the real surprise was that after the outrage, came forgiveness and then celebration. While Coke did lose its number one position to Pepsi in 1985, the re-launched Classic Coke regained leadership in 1986 and kept growing. New Coke faded away.

And the moral is that you need to take extra care when adapting classic brands. What are the negotiable and non-negotiable elements of your brand?

13 THE NOISY ENGINE AND THE QUIET CLOCK

In 1949, after working at a number of other agencies David Ogilvy left to help found a new agency. Ogilvy & Mather is today one of the largest advertising agencies in the world and part of the even larger WPP marketing services group. In 1953 Ogilvy & Mather won the prestigious Rolls Royce account and David Ogilvy and his team set about creating some new advertising for the brand.

Ogilvy believed in the importance of research and so immersed himself in the brand, its cars and its history. He avidly read all he could about how the cars were designed, how they were made and how they performed.

Several days into his research, he came cross a line in a technical report that stopped him in his tracks. It referred to some testing done on noise levels inside the car while travelling at various speeds. It was an unusual piece of information but one that he felt epitomized the superb engineering skills of the Rolls Royce engineers.

It read simply: "At 60 miles an hour, the loudest noise in the Rolls Royce was the ticking of the clock." David Ogilvy had not only discovered an intriguing, little known fact about the car's performance but had found a headline too!

And the moral is that it pays to interrogate your product until it squeaks. What is your product's true competitive advantage?

14 THE PARTY WITH EXTRA TOYS

In 1981, Ann Galea was working for Pippa Dee, a clothing company that sold its wares through parties organized in people's homes. She had just arranged for a party to take place in the front room of her house in Thamesmead, Essex, UK, when she had an idea. She decided to ask her friend, Jacqueline Gold, to bring along some of the merchandise from where Jacqueline worked.

Now, Jacqueline Gold's merchandise was more than a little unusual. She was working for her father's sex shop business at the time, so Galea asked Gold to bring along some sex toys, hoping it would spice up the event.

Looking back on the evening, Gold remembers: "It was like a Tupperware party, but at the end of the evening, out came the toys. The girls' reaction was amazing. Suddenly everyone was having fun and giggling. I could see there was a market."

Despite being just 21 and on work experience, Gold developed a radical business plan for what was at that time effectively an adult publishing and mail order company that happened to own a couple of shops. Her radical plan was based on selling sex toys to women in an environment where they would feel relaxed – at a party in a friend's house. Chatting to the women after the Pippa Dee party had made Jacqueline realize that, while women were just as interested in sex as men, they didn't want to visit or be seen to visit the sex shops of the time.

On hearing the plan, one Board member was supposedly outraged declaring "Women aren't interested in sex!", but thanks to support from her father and uncle, Gold's plan was given the go-ahead.

The first party organizers were recruited through advertising and seminars held in the Strand Palace hotel in London. "I had to tweak the ad," recalls Gold. "I couldn't say 'ladies only' and couldn't use 'erotic'; it had to be 'exotic'."

The first Ann Summer's Party generated £85 of sales. There are now some 7,500 party organizers who hold more than 4,000 parties every week. What's more, Gold no longer has to advertise for organizers. Applicants come to her.

With a successful online business, a chain of women-friendly sex shops on the UK high street and operations in Dubai and Australia, the brand's sales hit £117 million in 2012. As for the outraged Director, he may still be outraged, but he is no longer being so at Ann Summers!

And the moral is that if your customers won't come to you, go to your customers. What new channels could you use to connect with your customers?

15 THE AD THAT DIDN'T LIE

In 1961, the idea of an ad all about a faulty product must have seemed an unusual if not absurd idea. Yet an ad created that year featuring a faulty Volkswagen was to win a poll for the "World's Greatest Ad" nearly 40 years later.

Created by art director Helmut Krone and copywriter Julian Koenig of Doyle Dane Bernbach, the ad for the Volkswagen Beetle featured a black and white shot of the car and underneath it ran the forlorn, one-word headline: "Lemon".

The copy went on to detail how this particular Volkswagen failed the stringent quality checks. The chrome "fitting" around the glove compartment door was blemished and so the car was rejected by Kurt Kroner, one of 3,389 assembly plant workers at the Wolfsburg factory in Germany.

In a market awash with hyperbole and spin, it was an ad that was more honest; more truthful than those of its competitors. It was willing to admit the Beetle wasn't the most beautiful, the fastest or the most spacious car available. No, it was a small and, to many, an "ugly bug" of a car.

What the Beetle did have was its virtues of economy and

reliability. Combining these with humorous self-deprecation and a dash of honesty, it set about selling itself – and sell it did.

And the moral is that a great ad is often a truth well told. What truth should you be telling about your brand?

16 A MODEL BRAND, A MODEL BRAND MANAGER

Model, Actress, Presenter, Businesswoman and Pin-up she may be but Kelly Brook is much more than just a pretty face, she is a brand manager par excellence; and the brand she manages is the Kelly Brook brand.

Interviewed for *The Sunday Times* magazine she explains, "Ultimately, I'm not Kelly Brook, I'm Kelly Parsons." Parsons was the surname she was born with but which she dropped at 16 as her glamour modelling career started to take off. *"Kelly Brook is this thing I've created, it is me, but it's not me.*

"I sat down one day and wrote down everything I thought I would love in my fantasy life. If I wasn't Kelly Parsons, who had to pay the mortgage and get the train, if I was Kelly Brook all the time, what would that life be? Where would I live? What car would I drive? Where would I go on holiday? What make-up would I like? I wrote lists and lists.

"Then you give it to these branding people and they create this whole world. Once you've got that model and you understand what this brand is, what type of girls are going to like the

brand, what the demographic is, you can start thinking what products feed into that."

So what was on those lists? *"Polka dots, gingham, Marilyn Monroe, flowers...Being natural – I didn't do eyelashes or anything like that. I'm naturally booby, I've got naturally big hair."*

Like most good brand managers she pays attention to detail, constantly demands the quality she wants and is rightly passionate about her brand.

"You know that English mentality of 'Oh, that'll do'? That frustrates the hell out of me. I can get really upset about things that haven't been named correctly or colours that weren't what I wanted. I can be a spoilt brat, really. I get so passionate about stuff. Maybe sometimes the people here [at New Look, the fashion retailer she has been working with since 2012] *think, 'Oh, God, she's a nightmare', but that's because I care."*

And the moral is that every brand needs a passionate brand manager. Are the people working on your brand really committed to it?

17 A LITTLE WEIRDNESS GOES A LONG WAY

Dan Wieden is an adman and as such is a natural storyteller. One of his favourite stories relates to the creation of one of the world's most famous advertising end-lines and illustrates the benefits of "incorporating a little weirdness into the creative process".

The line in question is Nike's, and the weirdness is the source of inspiration for that line – the last words of a murderer, Gary Gilmore, who was executed in 1977.

In 1988, Dan was working on a new campaign for Nike and, while he and his team had decided on a series of clips of different athletes from different sports, the problem was that the campaign lacked an end-line and the presentation to an expectant client was fast approaching.

Working late into the night, Weiden suddenly found himself thinking about Gary Gilmore.

"So it's the middle of the night, and I'm sitting at my desk and I'm thinking about how Gilmore died. This was in Utah, and they dragged Gilmore out in front of the firing squad. Before they put the hood over his head, the chaplain asks Gilmore if he has any last words. And Gilmore pauses and he says 'Let's do it'.

"And I remember thinking, 'That is so fucking courageous'. Here is this guy calling for his own death.

"And then the next thing I know I'm thinking about my shoe commercials. I didn't like the way it was said, actually, so I made it a little different. I wrote 'Just Do It' on a piece of paper and as soon as I saw it, I knew. That was my slogan."

And the moral is that inspiration sometimes strikes when you least expect it. What could you do to take your mind off a problem and let you mind wander?

18 THE AGENCY THAT SAID "NO"

"Would you like to pitch for the Bacardi account?" It's a question that just about every advertising agency would surely like to hear. And if you were a relatively new agency it would be music to your ears, wouldn't it? The opportunity to pitch for a £7-8 million blue-chip account must be a chance too good to miss.

So it came as something of a surprise to Bacardi when the fledgling agency HHCL+Partners said no. There were no conflicts and the agency wasn't anti-alcohol or tee-total, yet despite being asked again HHCL continued to say no.

Based on a set of principles and the reputation of its founders, HHCL had been established in 1986 and soon established a name for itself as an agency that created distinctive and provocative advertising. One of those principles was that, as a small agency, it would close for new business if it felt it was growing so fast that it needed to "bed down" new clients and recruit new staff. It didn't want to over-stretch itself. It didn't want to over-promise and under-deliver.

The Bacardi call came during one of these periods and, even though they were sorely tempted, HHCL stuck to its principles and continued to say no. It turned its back on the chance to pitch for a highly prestigious and valuable account. It was unusual behaviour for an agency.

David Webey, the Bacardi client, was surprised but impressed. "If that's the level of service your current clients get, I want to be one."

Six months later, when HHCL had reopened its doors for new business, it was given another of the company's brands, Martini, without a pitch, and David Webey became a client.

And the moral is that a principle isn't a principle until it costs you money (but in the long run, remember that it will probably make you money). What are the principles to which your brand will stay true, even when tempted to do otherwise?

19 THE HAMBURGERS THAT DIDN'T GET BURNT

In 1992, the acquittal of the police officers accused of beating up Rodney King sparked the worst riots that Central South Los Angeles had ever witnessed. The local population were caught up in a wave of looting, rioting and burning that saw cars and houses destroyed.

Businesses were also destroyed – windows smashed, goods and merchandise looted and then the buildings were torched. Yet amongst all this destruction, the five McDonald's restaurants in the riot and fire zone escaped unscathed.

It was vindication of a policy that founder Ray Kroc had always advocated: "We believe a business should put something back into a community and that this pays dividends"; advice that the five franchise holders had followed. As Chuck Ebeling, then Director of Corporate Communications for McDonald's, recalled some years later:

"In the area of South Central LA, a five-square miles radius of devastation, the outcome was like a bomb. It resembled Nagasaki. Buildings had been looted and set alight. It was martial law. The streets were dangerous. Many people were killed in the frenzy, either as a statement of opposition between the established powers and the disenfranchised or as a gateway for much deeper held sentiments regarding race, class, poverty and divisions between the entitled and disentitled.

"In the wasted landscape of South Central LA, everything had been destroyed. Everything except for five buildings. In the post-apocalyptic aftermath, surrounded by smoldering ruins and debris, there were five buildings which had been untouched. Not a broken window. Not a slash of spray paint. All flooded in their usual operable fluoro lights.

"These five buildings all had one thing in common. They were all McDonald's."

Months later, sociologists at Stanford University came across this data. They were also intrigued. They sent teams into the field to get to the bottom of the phenomenon. They went in to interview many of those who had been involved in the riots. They went in to discover what the story was; not why the devastation had taken place, but why it hadn't taken place at McDonald's.

When asked why McDonald's was spared, the answers were the same across all interview centres. The general conversations went something like this:

"They are one of us."

"What do you mean?"
"They're looking after us."
"How could McDonald's be looking after you?"
"Because we like to play basketball. There's nothing else to do except get high and shit. McDonald's gives us balls."

It turned out that McDonald's had in fact supplied a number of basketballs to youth groups and basketball centres in these low socio-economic areas. Not thousands of balls. A few hundred.

"And the old men. My old man. They don't have jobs or nothin'. They don't have nowhere to live. McDonald's gives them free coffee."

It was true. In that area, McDonald's supplied several hundred free cups of coffee each morning. In terms of its profitability, "it was a piss in the ocean".

The business benefit of such benevolent acts isn't always so apparent, but if anyone in McDonald's ever questions their importance, they are told Ray Kroc's words and shown a short video. It shows the mayhem that struck Los Angeles and tells the story of the restaurants that were left standing, left to conduct business as usual, when all around others were burnt out.

And the moral is that a brand is a unit of social currency and should play a role in the wider community. What does your brand contribute to the local or wider community in which it exists?

20 THE JEALOUS FRENCHMAN

When Baron Philippe de Rothschild came into his inheritance in 1923, he took control of the Mouton wine estates that his family had purchased 70 years earlier in 1853.

Although its production methods were of a high standard, even wines such as Mouton were viewed and sold as a commodity. Many rich Frenchmen drank whiskey with their meals, while in more modest restaurants wine was given away free in carafes. The challenge Baron Philippe faced was that the Mouton brand didn't really exist.

Driving down the N10 between Angoulème and Bordeaux in his Bugatti, Baron Philippe saw advertisements for new branded drinks such as St. Raphaël, Suze and Quinquina.

He was soon a jealous man. Why did these products gain greater respect and better margins than his glorious wines? He decided that something had to be done.

With hindsight, his idea seems simple and logical but at the time it created outrage within the conservative wine industry for its radicalism. The Baron was even accused of being part of a Bolshevik plot!

Until that point, wine was sold in bulk to merchants, who were free to mix and blend it to their own specifications, adding everything from other wines to red ink or Neopolitan dried blood. The baron's radical concept was that he should maintain control of his product – his brand – not only through its origin and production, but also through its presentation and sale in the marketplace.

He decided to bottle his own product, a process that he named simply enough "chateau bottling".

He then went about creating an image, commissioning Jean Carlu, a noted member of the Union des Artistes Modernes, to create a logo for Mouton estate wines. The now famous marque combining the ram's head and an arrow was born.

What these two initiatives did was to provide a clear and recognizable means by which consumers could guarantee the consistent quality and integrity of the product they bought.

Rothschild's innovative thinking in wine continued, with the creation of Mouton Cadet in 1928. In 1935 he added his own signature to the label for the first time as another guarantee; this time a personal guarantee of quality.

And the moral is that brands are a guarantee of quality. How closely do you monitor and control your product or service?

21 THE GOLDEN WEB

Toronto-based gold mining company Goldcorp was in trouble. Besieged by strikes and lingering debts in a contracting market, the company had terminated its mining operations.

Most analysts assumed that the company's 50-year-old mine in Red Lake, Ontario, was dying. Without evidence of substantial new gold deposits, Goldcorp was likely to fold.

Chief Executive Officer Rob McEwen refused to accept that the end was nigh. He took an unconventional approach and decided to break some of the unwritten rules of the mining industry. Instead of hiding the proprietary, and potentially very revealing, geological data, he decided to publish it on the Web for all to see. In total it was some 400 megabytes worth of information about the 55,000-acre property.

He challenged the world to do the prospecting. The "Goldcorp Challenge" made available a total of $575,000 in prize money to participants who submitted the best methods and estimates.

Within weeks, submissions from around the world were flooding into Goldcorp headquarters. There were entries from more than 1,000 virtual prospectors in some 50 different countries. There were entries from graduate students, management consultants, mathematicians, military officers and a virtual army of geologists.

"We had applied math, advanced physics, intelligent systems, computer graphics and organic solutions to inorganic problems. There were capabilities I had never seen before in the industry," said McEwen. "When I saw the computer graphics, I almost fell out of my chair."

The contestants identified 110 targets on the Red Lake property, more than 80% of which yielded substantial quantities of gold.

In the end 8 million ounces of gold have been found, worth well over $3 billion. (Not a bad return on a half-million dollar investment.)

The process also introduced Goldcorp to state-of-the-art technologies and exploration methodologies, and more advanced approaches to geological modelling. Goldcorp went from being an underperforming $100-million company to a $9-billion juggernaut. One hundred dollars invested in the company in 1993 is worth more than $3,000 today.

And the moral is that a fresh pair of eyes can bring a fresh perspective; 1,000 fresh pairs of eyes can open your eyes to lots of new opportunities. What problem could you outsource?

22 FLIPPING THE HARP

Arthur Guinness started brewing in Dublin in 1759. Within ten years one particular product, Guinness Extra Strong Porter, was being exported to England, where it became known as Guinness Stout.

By 1862, Guinness decided it needed to further develop its brand identity and chose the O'Neill harp as its icon. Also known as the Gaelic harp, the Celtic harp or the Brian Boru harp, the O'Neill harp has a long history dating back at least 1,000 years. Brian Boru, the last High King of Ireland, is said to have been an accomplished player and surviving 12th Century annals refer to the Celtic harp being the only instrument played during the Crusades.

It was seen as a perfect symbol of tradition, Irish-ness and enjoyment. The icon was trademarked in 1876.

All was well until 1922, when Ireland was declared an independent state and the Irish Free State Government decided it needed an official national symbol.

And the symbol it wanted was the traditional O'Neill harp.

Guinness, which by then had spent over 150 years building a powerful communication equity, was now faced with a dilemma: to go against the newly formed government or to give up their harp.

In the end, the answer was staring it in the face, at least when it was looking in the mirror. A bright spark suggesting flipping the harp and the Government readily agreed on a reversal. (Was this the first instance of a U-turn by an Irish Government?)

So to this day the Guinness harp always appears with its straight edge, the sound board, to the left, and the Government harp is always shown with its straight edge to the right.

The official Government harp is to be found on the Presidential Seal, on passports, on the flag of Leinster (but not the national flag), on Irish Euro coins and as a logo for a number of prominent state-supported organizations (such as the National University of Ireland).

And Guinness' harp remains as one of the three elements that make up the Guinness livery. The other two elements are the GUINNESS® word and Arthur Guinness' famous signature.

And the moral is that creating and managing your identity is a key responsibility for any management team. Are all the key elements of your identity protected?

23 THE POWER OF TWO LITTLE WORDS

Two little words were to cost Gerald Ratner several million pounds, his own job and those of many of his employees. It was also to result in a new term being added to the lexicon of marketing – *"Doing a Ratner".*

In 1984 Gerald Ratner had taken control of the jewellery business his father, Leslie, had founded 33 years earlier. Over the next few years he steadily built the company so that it became the UK's leading specialist retail jeweller.

His approach was to focus the business solely on retailing and to target the lower end of the market. He helped turn jewellery into a more regular purchase for the ordinary consumer rather than just a special or occasional one. Ratners was, for a number of years, a highly successful low-margin, high-volume business model.

Then in April 1991, Gerald Ratner was invited to speak at the Institute of Directors' annual conference. Believing that his audience would appreciate some humour in what was potentially a rather dry and worthy speech, he referred to one of the products they sold as *"total crap"*.

Unfortunately his comment wasn't seen as humorous or simply honest. Instead, people felt it represented a disdain for his customers. Worse still, it was immediately and widely reported in the media. Ratners was rechristened as "Crapners".

Customers responded by deserting the store in droves and sales fell dramatically. This, combined with an economic downturn and the company's high levels of debt, meant that the whole company quickly descended to a point where it nearly folded.

Ratners was forced to sell off some of its assets, including Watches of Switzerland, which was sold to Aspery's in June 1992. In November of that year, Gerald Ratner resigned as Chairman, his position having become untenable.

In September 1993, Ratners announced that it was changing its name to Signet and was switching its shop fasciae to Ernest Jones, H. Samuel or Signet.

Gerald Ratner wasn't the first and probably won't be the last to "Do a Ratner", but his name will be forever associated with the term used whenever a senior executive of a company makes a highly inappropriate or derogatory remark about their brand or their customers.

And the moral is that if you don't believe in your brand, why

should anyone else? Are you and your fellow employees true advocates for your brand?

24 THE STARS' FREE GIFTS

Trivial Pursuit was the board game of the 1980s. In 1984 it sold 20 million copies. A brilliantly simple idea based on our love of trivia and our love of friendly competition, with questions like:

What word was intentionally omitted from the screenplay of The Godfather*?* (Mafia)

How many rows of whiskers does a cat have? (Four)

Do you know what the other secret behind the success of Trivial Pursuit was?

The answer is word of mouth, that most powerful form of advertising. However, the owners didn't rely on that alone. They helped stoke the fire through the clever use of what is sometimes called "buzz" marketing.

They sent a series of single sample cards to key buyers attending Toy Fair 1983. The game itself and the purpose of the intriguing cards were only revealed on the third mailing.

Later, they gave free copies to radio stations which promised to use the questions as the basis of on-air competitions.

Linda Pezzano, the PR Manager on the launch of the game, remembers how the idea developed:

"In New York there was a guy on the radio who loved to ask trivia questions, so I thought he was a natural guy to do a promotion with. And then I thought, 'Well there must be guys like that in every market'."

So Pezzano hired a student to call up the different stations and identify their "trivia" disc jockeys. Soon, over 100 stations were running Trivia Pursuit competitions. Taking this idea a stage further, sample cards were offered to bars that agreed to host trivia parties.

One final twist saw free copies of the game sent to the celebrities who were mentioned in the questions or answers. "The celebrity mailing turned a lot of opinion leaders to the game, and they loved it," recalls Pezzano.

And the moral is that (to quote Bill Bernbach) word of mouth is the best form of advertising. What could you do to generate positive word of mouth?

25 THE PLASTIC PEOPLE WITH THE PLASTIC SMILES

Oxo is the leading stock cube brand in the UK and has been so for nearly 100 years. However, despite a history of great advertising, in the early 1980s it had lost its edge. Unfortunately for the brand this was just at the time when it was facing an increasing difficult marketplace.

There was a general decline in meat eating, a rapid increase in the consumption of ethnic foods (not something with which Oxo was generally associated), growth in the cooking-sauce market and on-going competition from other stock cube and gravy granule brands.

J. Walter Thompson, Oxo's advertising agency, and its senior planner, Ev Jenkins, suggested a radical piece of research. The research wouldn't focus on a new campaign idea, or even the brand itself, but would investigate family life in the UK. It would explore what family life was really like in the 1980s and what people's reactions were to how families were being presented in the media. While such ethnographic research is now commonplace, it was the first time that a major brand had commissioned a study that went beyond the scope of its business.

Ev Jenkins' rationale was that Oxo should be positioned as being central to good home cooking, and that good home cooking was central to good home life. This atypical research was conducted by Stephen Wells and he recalls:

"When I asked these mothers about family life, they let loose with a deluge of the trials and tribulations of everyday family life – doing the washing, trying to dry it when it had rained every day, doing the shopping and still trying to make ends meet, working out what to cook and then trying to get the kids to eat...

"Then, just as I was wondering why anyone had a family if this is what it was really like, one of the mothers would

remember something heart-warming – their child's first steps, a drawing brought home from school, and suddenly everyone would be smiling."

This uneven balance of grief offset with small but very precious moments of relief was the reality of family life. Stephen christened it "war and peace" but noted "that there seemed to a lot more war than peace".

The second key finding was that in the early 1980s, UK broadcast media were moving ahead of advertising. Programmes such as *Butterflies*, which humorously depicted a mother's attempts to cope with two teenage sons, and the soap *Brookside* were starting to reflect the reality of everyday life much more honestly than advertising.

Advertising of the time was full of perfect families, made up of attractive mums, handsome dads, and children who were always immaculately behaved. Someone in the research christened them "plastic people with plastic smiles".

What the research clearly identified was that there was an opportunity for a brand to reflect more accurately what family life was like. Based on these two key insights, JWT developed what was to become one of the most famous and effective food advertising campaigns of all time. Launched in 1983, it ran until 1999.

And the moral is that advertising doesn't need to be glossy to be successful; empathy is a powerful tool. How well do you really know the motivations and realities of your customers?

26 BATMAN AND THE BALL BOYS

In the summer of 1989, the UK launch of Tim Burton's *Batman* movie was the big cinema news. Yet despite the multi-million pound marketing campaign, one of its most successful promotional activities cost little more than a few hundred pounds and a dash of creative thinking.

The film was scheduled for launch in late June; early summer in the UK and the time when the British traditionally get interested in tennis and eat lots of strawberries and cream – time for the Wimbledon tennis championship. The event has been covered by BBC TV for many years; a terrestrial state-run channel that doesn't take any advertising. That being the case, it doesn't present itself as the most obvious promotional opportunity. However, the marketing team for the film came up with a little wheeze that was to get around this minor problem.

They had a few hundred t-shirts printed with a large Batman logo across the chests. Then they stood outside the gates and offered a new t-shirt to everyone entering, on one small condition – they must put it on immediately.

Hundreds of tennis fans eagerly accepted their free gift and promptly donned their shirts.

TV coverage of the match went on as normal, with the camera moving from side to side as the ball flew over the net. But at the end of the rally when the camera turned to the crowds for a reaction shot, there were the mass ranks of people all wearing the Batman logo.

It was fantastic exposure worth literally hundreds of thousands of pounds but achieved at almost no cost.

And the moral is that sometimes you can out-think rather than out-spend your competition. Instead of wishing for a bigger budget, ask yourself what you would do if your advertising and promotion spend were cut in half.

27 THE TIGER AND THE COMMITTEE

Joe Rohde, the Head Imagineer on the Animal Kingdom project for Disneyland, Florida, was beginning to think that his team would never get the final go-ahead on their $1-billion enterprise.

CEO Michael Eisner was in favour, but many of the strategic planners weren't so sure. It was the late 1980s, the economy was slipping into recession and the existing Disney theme park business was suffering. Animal Kingdom was a project that would be five times bigger than the original Disneyland in California.

Meeting after meeting had taken place over a number of

months, but Joe was getting nowhere fast. The planners still weren't convinced; they didn't believe that the idea was a significant improvement on a traditional zoo.

Some of their scepticism rubbed off on Michael Eisner, who at one of their meetings wondered aloud whether the mere sight of live animals would generate enough excitement and interest amongst their guests.

Joe called together his team of Imagineers – the eclectic bunch of designers, artists, writers and engineers who help to create the Disney magic. He wanted to work out a plan to get the committee of planners to change their minds.

At the next meeting Joe took along an accomplice to help him argue the case – but his accomplice wasn't just anyone; it was a live animal, a "mere" 400-pound Bengal tiger.

Perhaps not surprisingly, the planners quickly realized how much interest and excitement live animals can generate. Joe and the team got their go-ahead ... and in 1998, Disney opened its new Animal Kingdom theme park.

And the moral is that even the most hardened professional is a human, and the use of theatre can be a powerful decision-making tool. How can you dramatize your next presentation?

28 SOME BINS AND SOME FRUIT

Within the marketing fraternity, certain brands seem to get a disproportionate amount of attention. In the 80s and 90s it was Virgin, but in the noughties it was innocent. The brand was founded by three friends, all Cambridge University graduates: Richard Reed, Adam Balon and Jon Wright. It's strange to think that one of the most talked about and successful brands of the last decade nearly didn't get started. In fact, the original partners weren't completely convinced by their own market research and the decision to proceed came down to the flip of a coin. Richard Reed tells the story on www.inc.com:

"In February 1998 we were three 26-year-old friends living together and working in London, and we'd always wanted to set up a business together and we'd try to think up ideas. We were drinking too much beer and eating too much pizza and we thought we'd solve the riddle of healthy eating – everyone knows the benefits of it, but modern life conspires against it. So we thought totally natural fruit smoothies would be a great little healthy habit and would make it easy for people to do themselves some good.

"After about six months we had this orange, banana and pineapple recipe, and we needed to test it on people other than our friends and family, who of course all said it was good.

"So we bought £500 of fruit and set up a stall at the Jazz on the Green festival in Parsons Green, which we thought would be full of the type of people who'd buy our product.

"Originally we had a three-page market research form for people to fill out, but when it's a lovely sunny day you don't want to fill out a form. And it felt too corporate. And so someone said: 'Don't you just want to know if people will buy them or not?' So we had a sign that said: 'Do you think we should give up our jobs to make these smoothies?' and we had a 'yes' bin and a 'no' bin, and we committed to each other that if the yes bin was full we'd quit our jobs the next day.

"And the yes bin was full, but still we weren't sure. So we went back to our house in Barons Court and flipped a coin, and it came up three times in a row tails.

"So we all went in Monday morning and resigned."

And the rest, as they say, is history.

And the moral is that market research doesn't need complicated methodologies to be useful. Could you simplify or reduce the amount of research you do and still get the information you truly need?

29 IT TAKES ALL SORTS

Charlie Robertson was getting worried. His pitch wasn't going well. He had been through almost the entire Bassett's portfolio of sweets and his potential client hadn't seemed interested in a single one.

Exasperated, he turned round to get his last few samples, but in doing so he knocked over a whole range of his jars. The storekeeper took one look at the resulting higgledy-piggledy mixture of all the different sorts of liquorice-based sweets and much to Charlie's surprise and great delight, immediately placed a large order for the mix.

The year was 1899 and Bassett's Liquorice Allsorts[2] were born. Orders are still pouring in.

And the moral is that serendipity can be a source of innovation. Does your innovation process allow for chance and the wild card?

30 THE STITCHING AND THE E-MAIL

Nike iD was set up to allow its customers to personalize their trainers. For a small surcharge, you could choose between a range of colours and select your own lettering, which would duly appear under the famous Nike swoosh.

"If you want it done, build it yourself," proclaimed the website. It seemed the perfect solution in an era that saw an ever-increasing demand for individuality. Offering customization seemed another way of allowing consumers to *"Just do it".* Nike was in effect giving them control over "their" product.

---

2 The Bassett brand's "mascot" is Bertie Bassett, a figure made up entirely of liquorice allsorts and launched in 1929.

All seemed well until an American student by the name of Johan Perretti asked for the word "Sweatshop" to be stitched into his trainers. It was a clear reference to the very public stories of Nike's use of cheap child labour in South East Asia.

It seemed like it could be a potential PR disaster, so Nike took swift action. To avoid bad PR, Nike simply refused Johan Perretti's request, citing his use of "profanity or inappropriate slang".

They hoped the matter would be closed. It wasn't. An interchange of emails followed, with Peretti challenging the logic of this decision and Nike refusing to shift.

Finally, Peretti accepted Nike's right to veto his choice of word, asking only that Nike send him *"a colour snapshot of the ten -year-old Vietnamese girl who makes my shoes".*

Unsurprisingly, Peretti never received a response to this final request. Instead, he copied the whole interchange to friends and acquaintances. From there, it was received and forwarded by many thousands of people on the Net, one of whom noted the correspondence went *"round the world much further and faster than any of the adverts they paid Michael Jordan more than the entire wage packet of all their sweatshop workers in the world to do".*

And the moral is that social media opens out a world of possibilities – but these aren't always positive. Have you thought through all the implications of your social media strategy?

31 THE SPELLING MISTAKE, THE BACKRUB AND 100 ZEROS

Here's a story you can backrub – sorry, Google.

Google founders Larry Page and Sergey Brin met at Stanford University in 1995. By 1996, they had built a search engine that used links to determine the importance of individual webpages. Their name for the fledgling product was *"Backrub".*

On reflection, Brin and Page decided that perhaps Backrub wasn't such a good name. It was certainly unusual and original, but they wanted something that related in some way to the service they aimed to provide in linking millions of webpages together.

After much consideration, they chose a word for a huge number: a 'Googol'. A googol is the term for the number represented by 1 followed by 100 zeros.

Brin and Page liked it so much because it truly reflected the scale of their ambition.

It also fitted with what was to become their mission statement: *"To organize the world's information and make it universally accessible and useful."*

However, the name was to undergo one further and unexpected change.

One of their first investors was farsighted enough to see the potential in what they wanted to do, but his spelling wasn't quite as good as his business sense. When he wrote out his cheque, he made it out to "Google".

Brin and Page liked it and the new name stuck.

And the moral is that not all mistakes produce bad results. Looking back over mistakes you may have made in the past, how can you capitalize on something that went wrong?

32 THE LIPSTICK AND THE AIRLINE

While many in marketing know the story of how Post-it notes came to be (see page 92), the story of another sticky innovation is equally engaging.

Wolfgang Zengerling, former Head Archivist at Henkel AG, says that the inspiration for the world's first glue stick came from an airline flight.

The story goes that one of Henkel's chemists, who was working in the adhesives business, was travelling to a meeting on a plane. Sitting next to him was a woman who, as they came into land, started to put on her make-up. The chemist was intrigued and watched her closely.

He was particularly fascinated by the way she applied her

lipstick. He watched her twist the bottom of the tube to push the lipstick up and just over the top, letting her apply it easily to her lips. No fuss, no messy colour on her hands, and a nice, smooth, even finish.

The proverbial light bulb went off as he saw immediately how the application of glue could be made easier. How you could ensure you wouldn't end up with glue on your hands or on any surfaces other than those you wished to stick, and how you would get a nice smooth application.

Pritt Stick, the world's first glue stick, was launched in 1969 and is still going strong in 34 countries.

And the moral is that inspiration can strike at anytime, anywhere. Are you constantly curious, always attuned to looking for new ideas?

33 THE BANK THAT LIKES TO SAY NO

ING Direct (USA) was launched in September 2000. From the start it liked to do things differently.

"One way or another, most financial companies are telling you to spend more. We're showing you how to save more," said original CEO Arkadi Kuhlmann.

ING is an Internet-based savings bank, dealing directly with its customers. It has only a limited number of easy-to-understand products. It prides itself on speed, simplicity and low overheads. It claims to be the bank for the people on "Main Street, not Wall Street".

But it says no to what a lot of other banks like to say yes to.

There are NO minimum deposits and NO customers' fees. It has NO ATMs, NO branches, NO advisors (it's an Internet, virtually paperless organization). It doesn't market checking accounts or auto loans. Not only does it not market credit cards, ING openly campaigns against them

"If you're truly committed to helping people change their financial lives and to doing it step by step, then you should not encourage them to do things that could lead them to lose money," says Chief Customer Service Officer Jim Kelly.

In one famous instance, ING turned down a wealthy potential customer who wanted to deposit $5 million with the bank. It was nothing personal, it said, but: "Rich Americans are used to platinum cards, special service – the last thing we want in this bank is to have rich people making special demands. We treat everyone the same."

The business also "fires" around 3,500 customers a year who don't play by their rules – making too many calls to customer service, or asking for too many exceptions to procedures.

ING expects and accepts the consequences: "The customers who are right for you, they have you. They become evangelists. The customers who close out, they hate you. But you know what they do when they hate you? They tell everyone about you – and that's good. It creates dialogue. There's nothing like differentiation," says Kuhlmann.

The result of their approach? By 2004, the business was making a pre-tax profit of $250 million per annum.

And the moral is that it can pay to zig when the world zags. Is there an opportunity in doing the opposite of what all your competitors are doing?

34 BROTHERLY LOVE?

Christoph Dassler worked in a shoe factory. He had two sons, Adolf and Rudolf.

Returning from World War I, the brothers went different ways. Adolf – known as Adi – kept the family's interest in shoes going and began producing his own sports shoes in his mother's wash kitchens. Meanwhile Rudolf, or "Rudi", took up a management position at a porcelain factory, later joining a leather wholesale business.

Rudi returned to their hometown of Herzogenaurach in July 1924 and joined his younger brother's business. It was renamed the Gebrüder Dassler Schuhfabrik (Dassler Brothers Shoe Factory) and began to prosper.

With the 1936 Summer Olympics in Germany pending, Adi spotted an opportunity. He travelled to the Olympic

Village with a suitcase full of their shoe spikes, and there persuaded US sprinter Jesse Owens to use them. It was the first commercial sponsorship of an African American.

When Owens won four gold medals, the reputation of Dassler shoes rose. Letters from around the world landed on the brothers' desks, as sportsmen and coaches of other national teams became interested in their shoes. Business boomed, and by the late 1930s the Dasslers were selling some 200,000 pairs of shoes a year.

Like most brothers, Adi and Rudi had many arguments, but it was during the course of the World War II that they were to fall out. Though both brothers joined the Nazi party, relationships were strained, and reached breaking point during a bomb attack in 1943.

Rudi and his family were sitting in a bomb shelter when Adi and his wife arrived. Rudi heard his brother say: "The dirty bastards are back again."

Thinking that Adi was referring to him, and not to the Allied war planes, Rudi was furious. The row worsened when Rudi was picked up by American soldiers and accused of being a member of the Waffen SS. He was convinced that his brother had turned him in. The brothers split in 1947.

Rudi formed a new firm that he initially called Ruda – a *worger* (word merger) of Rudolf Dassler – later rebranded Puma, while Adi formed Adidas AG. While it is sometimes claimed that the name is an acronym for "All Day I Dream About Sport", the name is actually another *worger* of "Adi" and "Das(sler)".

The rivalry between the two businesses was fierce and bitter. Herzogenaurach was equally split, and acquired a new nickname: "the town of bent necks", referring to the townspeople's habit of forever looking down to check which brand of shoes strangers were wearing.

So much for brotherly love!

And the moral is that competition is often good for both parties. How can you use your competition to your advantage?

35 THE WOMAN OF MANY FACES

She has been writing recipes since the 1920s, has appeared on countless radio stations and has had her portrait painted on numerous occasions over the years – but like Dorian Gray, she doesn't seem to age and in fact often appears younger than she did in earlier portraits.

She, or at least her picture, has been brought into just about every household in the US and many more across the world. In 1945, she was the best known woman in the US next to Eleanor Roosevelt.

Her name is Betty Crocker, and she doesn't really exist.

Betty's birth, if you can call it that, can be traced back to a promotion run by the Gold Medal flour brand in 1921.

The promotion allowed people to "win" a pin cushion in the shape of a flour sack.

Along with their entries, thousands of people sent in questions about their baking problems. The advertising manager at the time, Sam Gale, decided it would be good PR to answer the questions, but felt that it would be more appropriate and believable for responses to come from a woman. So Betty Crocker was born, in the form of a signature.

In 1924, she acquired a voice and appeared on the radio for the first time. In 1936, her portrait was painted for the first time, and by 1941 she was known to nine out of ten American housewives.

20 years on from there, Betty Crocker's *New Picture Cookbook* offered its readers advice such as: "Think pleasant thoughts while working and a chore will become a labour of love". Fast-forward another 25 years and the focus of her cookbook became time-saving in the kitchen and producing "lively meals".

The Betty Crocker brand name still appears on over 100 different products, while her appearance continues to change with the times.

For an advertising campaign in the 1990s, photographs of 75 different Becky Crocker users were taken and blended together to create a single, more modern and hopefully realistic image for the brand icon. She truly is a woman of many faces.

And the moral is that people like people, making

personification a powerful branding tool. How can you give your brand a human face?

36 MORE THAN A PROMISE

It was 1962 and Robert C. Townsend had a problem. He had just been appointed president of Avis, a company that had spent the last 13 years in the red.

Townsend recognized that Avis needed a new start and a more positive image. So he hired hotshot advertising agency Doyle Dane Bernbach (DDB) to help him turn things around. However, he knew that more was needed than a clever gimmicky line; he would need a powerful business philosophy that every Avis employee would then need to deliver.

Townsend agreed that prior to creating any ads, DDB would spend time learning about Avis' business; meeting, watching, talking and listening to Avis employees about the company and the way it did business.

It was during one of the early meetings that a deceptively simple question was asked: "Why does anybody ever rent a car from you?" The reply would go on to help make advertising history: "We try harder because we have to."

DDB's Art Director, Helmut Krone, had already decided that he wanted to centre the campaign on the blunt truth that "Avis is only No. 2". It was copywriter Paula Green who remembered what she had learned during those first research meetings and teamed it with the now-famous phrase: "We try harder".

Having identified the core idea, the DDB team developed the whole campaign as expressions of frank and truthful statements about Avis' business philosophy.

However, true to his belief that Avis needed more than just a clever piece of advertising, Robert Townsend and the entire management team travelled to every branch in America and spoke with every single employee. They explained that the success of the campaign, and more importantly of their business, hinged upon providing superior customer service at every chance they got.

The advertising was a promise; it was their responsibility to deliver on that promise. In just one year, the campaign and the employee commitment to delivering on it literally changed the fortunes of the company.

Prior to the campaign starting in 1963, Avis' revenue was $34 million and losses were $3.2 million. One year later, revenue had jumped to $38 million and for the first time in 13 years, Avis turned a profit of $1.2 million. Avis' market share grew from 11% in 1962 to 35% in 1966.

And the moral is that a brand is more than a promise, it's a responsibility. Are you making sure that you live up to your responsibilities?

37 THE INCISIVE LETTER K

Naming, whether it's a child or a brand, is a difficult business. In the end, it's more subjective than objective, so it's not surprising that there are many and varied strategies for choosing a name.

The most common approach is simply to take the name of the founder or founders. Birdseye and Woolworths are two from opposite ends of the alphabet. However, even with this most simple of approaches there are variations on the theme; while there was indeed a Mr Brooke, he invented his fictional partner Mr Bond, because he thought Brooke Bond sounded so good.

"Worgers" – or word mergers – are another favourite. Two appropriate words are taken and squashed together to create a new word. As an example, when Hasbro launched a new game in which players drew pictures of words to try to communicate their meaning, the company merged *"picture"* and *"dictionary" to create "Pictionary".*

Ole Kirk Christiansen merged two Danish words: *"leg godt"*, meaning *"play well"* to create Lego. At the time, he was unaware that in Latin *"lego"* means "I build".

When he introduced his first camera in June 1888, however, George Eastman decided he wouldn't follow either of these routes. He wanted a name that meant nothing.

"I devised the name myself...I knew that a brand name had

to be short, vigorous, incapable of being misspelled to an extent that would destroy its identity and, in order to satisfy trademark, it must mean nothing.

"The letter K had been a favourite with me – it seems a strong, incisive sort of letter. Therefore, the word I wanted had to start with a K. It became a question of trying out a great number of combinations of letters that made words starting and ending with K. The word Kodak was the result."

And the moral is that creativity thrives on a tight brief. Do you make sure every creative brief you write has clear and tight guidelines to guide the thinking and help your assessment of the work?

38 THE MEERKATS, THE COMPETITION AND A HEALTHY DOSE OF NECESSITY

Sometimes the hand you are dealt in marketing doesn't seem that attractive when you first look at it, and in the UK comparethemarket.com didn't seem to have too much going for it in the beginning.

It had been one of the last to market, was fourth in category of four and so a small player in a category where size matters. The bigger you are in comparison insurance sites, the better. You need awareness and you need people to visit you – as visiting you is in your case the equivalent for them of visiting dozens of other sites. The traditional way to size is through advertising spend or differentiation.

Unfortunately, research found that the name comparethemarket.com was relatively unmemorable and was in fact very similar to its nearest and bigger spending competitor – gocompare.com.

Comparethemarket.com also had no single feature on which it could build a point of difference, meaning that it had to approach its marketing in a very different way.

At the time, comparison site advertising was all very similar: computer screens, cars with stars on them and claims galore – "You could save up to £300", "We compare more insurers than anybody else", "The price you see is the price you pay", "Almost everybody in the country could save £XXX"...

And they shouted it very loudly: four major players shared around 1,500 TV spots a day. Not surprisingly, despite how good the product was, the advertising was lousy and everyone hated it. The opportunity wasn't therefore a traditional USP – a unique selling proposition – but a new kind of USP: a unique selling persona. Comparethemarket decided to try and do something different; to create insurance comparison site advertising that would be entertaining and would be liked.

It drew inspiration from other insurance brands, not its direct competition in comparison sites but older standard insurance brands which had built awareness and even affection by creating and using icons. Admiral, Churchill, Direct Line all had warmer personalities depicted by people, animals and animated objects.

The final part of the inspirational jigsaw was necessity –

sometimes called the mother of invention. If comparison sites want to keep costs down, they have to get people to type in their brand name. Google charges less if people search by brand name; it charges more if they search for something generic like "car insurance" or "market". Comparethemarket needed to find a way of side-stepping the high cost per click on the generic word *"market"* (over £5).

It needed a cheaper term or phrase in its advertising that could exist alongside "market" and encourage people to use the brand name.

The answer was Meerkats.

And while it took a little while for Aleksandr Orlov to catch on, this complex, affection and traffic-generating character frustrated by the confusion between Comparethemarket.com and Comparethemeerkat.com, is now established as an advertising icon.

An icon with some impressive results to his name too: his first campaign achieved its 12-month objectives in nine weeks, and the brand is now number one in spontaneous awareness and consideration. Cost per visit was reduced by 73%, while quote volumes increased by over 83%.

And the moral is that you don't have to be first to market to succeed (though perhaps being first to meerkat did help). What do you need to do to make a late entry into the market distinctive and compelling?

39 DADDY'S GOOD LUCK CHARM

The day after Christmas 1944, Kevin Bell left this family's Oaktown farm for the World War II battlefields of the Pacific. In his duffel bag, along with his clothes and some personal things, he took six bottles of Coke.

The first time he got homesick, he drank one as it reminded him of life back on the farm. He shared four more with fellow soldiers whilst in Burma.

And the last bottle?
Well, he never opened it. He carried it back to the farm, where it sat for more than 30 years on the mantelpiece in the living room.

When the farmhouse caught fire in 1990, Kevin, by then an old man, rescued it from the burning building – one of the only material possessions he fought to save.

Kevin has since passed away, but his daughter Iris Bell keeps the bottle on her kitchen counter. "Daddy always said it was a good-luck charm, so I keep it here and my daughters will get it when I'm gone."

And the moral is that great brands make emotional as well as functional connections. What emotion does your brand evoke?

40 M IS FOR MOM'S NIGHT OFF

The Golden Arches are one of the most instantly recognized brand icons in the world. They were originally real arches and part of the restaurant design guidelines.

They were first introduced in 1953 but by the mid-1960s there was debate as to whether or not the Arches should be dropped.

Louis Cheskin, a designer and psychologist, who worked with McDonald's at the time, agreed that it might be sensible to move away from them as an architectural feature, but he argued strongly and ultimately successfully that "the arches had Freudian applications to the subconscious mind of the consumer and were great assets in marketing McDonald's food".

He went on to say that the arches were seen as "mother McDonald's breasts, a useful association if you're replacing home-made food".

In fact, "Give Mom a Night Off" had been an early advertising slogan, as a trip to McDonald's meant no cooking, serving or washing up.

The stylized M is still part of the logo to this day, and presumably those useful associations remain.

And the moral is that people react to messaging both rationally and emotionally, on a conscious and a subconscious level. What are people really taking out from your communications?

41 GOOD LUCK'S BAD LUCK

Eleanor Roosevelt had a most impressive CV. She was First Lady of the United States from 1933 to 1945, supporting her husband President Franklin D. Roosevelt and his New Deal policies.

After her husband's death in 1945, Roosevelt continued to be an internationally prominent author, speaker, politician and activist. She worked tirelessly to enhance the status of working women, though she opposed the Equal Rights Amendment because she believed it would adversely affect women.

She was a delegate to the UN General Assembly from 1945 to 1952, a role in which she chaired the committee that drafted and approved the Universal Declaration of Human Rights. President Truman called her the "First Lady of the World", in tribute to her human rights achievements.

So when this colossus of a woman was asked to endorse a brand, you might have thought that nothing could go wrong. Unfortunately for all concerned, it wasn't her finest hour.

In a TV commercial for Good Luck Margarine, she told viewers that: "The new Good Luck margarine really tastes delicious". She was paid the then handsome fee of $35,000 for her troubles. Sadly, the results weren't great for either the company or herself.

Looking back on it, she said with her normal forthright honesty and wit, that she had received a postbag full of letters in which *"one half was sad because I'd damaged my reputation;*

the other half was happy because I'd damaged my reputation".

And the moral is that celebrity-based advertising affects both the celebrity and the brand. If you use a celebrity, will they add value both to your proposition and to their own?

42 10

Sometimes less is more, and as the old adage suggests, it can pay to "Keep It Simple Stupid" – though few people would call Tesco stupid after the success it has had in the last 15 years.

Sir Terry Leahy,[3] CEO for much of this period, has attributed a major part of the brand's success to keeping it simple, with Tesco's ten-word vision.

In 1997, Sir Terry Leahy and the other directors met. After much discussion, they came up with the ten words that were to shape the future of the business:

"To create value for customers to earn their lifetime loyalty."

They also came up with two of what they called "values", to support and communicate to all their employees how

3 Sir Terry Leahy clearly likes the number ten. After stepping down from Tesco he wrote a business book called *Management in Ten Words*, in which he says he draws on his experience to pinpoint the ten vital attributes that make successful managers and underlie great organizations. Each chapter focuses on a single word (and indeed are the sorts of single words you find used by many of the Fortune 500/FTSE100 firms to describe their values.) They are Truth, Loyalty, Courage, Values, Act, Balance, Simple, Lean, Compete and Trust.

they wanted to deliver the vision. Unlike many other organizations, their values weren't standard single words such as "trusted", "caring", "quality" or "innovative".

Instead, they were sentences. Though they now seem quite generic, these sentences did and do provide guidance on how the organization and its people should act. They represent the stimulus that will drive customers' reactions to the brand, not just the responses they want to engender.

The two sentences were: "No one tries harder for customers" and "Treat people how we like to be treated". In the following decades Tesco expanded into Europe and Asia, financial services and telecommunications, but the core purpose, values and strategy didn't change.

As Leahy said, in a speech nearly a decade later, "The bigger you are, the more important it is that you have a clear vision and a set of values that everyone understands and lives by."

And the moral is that a clear vision and set of values should be at the core of your brand. Are yours clearly defined and known throughout the organization?

43 NO FRILLS BUT LOTS OF LAUGHS

In 1967 Texas businessman Rollin King and lawyer Herb Kelleher founded Air Southwest. It was an interstate airline linking Dallas, Houston and San Antonio. In 1971 the company changed its name to Southwest Airlines and made its first scheduled flight.

Its aims were relatively straightforward: low fares, high frequency flights and a dedication to its staff and customers. Its business model was unusual for the time – the airline concentrated on short-haul flights using less congested smaller airports and more direct routes. For example, in 1972 it moved all Houston flights to Hobby Airport from Houston International.

"After all, why should our customers have to drive 45 minutes to take a 40-minute flight?" asked Herb Kelleher at the time.

It used only of one type of aircraft which helped the company minimize training and maintenance costs.

It offered low-priced fares, with only a single class and no re-allocated seats.

At the time this was all pretty revolutionary but was to become the model for almost all the low-cost airlines around the world.

However, there was one further thing that differentiated Southwest Airlines and that was its own brand of "in-flight entertainment".

Attendants were encouraged to be themselves and have fun at work. A "typical" announcement might be: *"This is a non-smoking flight. Federal law prohibits smoking on board and in the aircraft's toilets ... However, passengers wishing to smoke will be invited to our special lounge situated on the wing where they will be able to view their own in-flight movie* – Gone with the Wind."

The results were outstanding. Over the 70s and 80s the airline steadily built its operation adding more cities and gaining more passengers – passing 5 million in 1975, and flying 9.5 million customers in 1983, 13 million in 1986 to now handle over 60 million passengers a year. Nowadays it has 2,700 daily flights to more than 55 cities in 29 states.

Southwest Airlines sums up its approach as: *"If you get your passengers to their destinations when they want to get there, on time, at the lowest possible fares and make darn sure they have a good time doing it, people will fly your airline".*

And the moral is that a little humour can go a long way. What are you doing that will put a smile on your customers' faces?

44 THE NO SCOLD GUARANTEE

One day in 1914, in a small Japanese town, a little boy called Soichiro saw a noisy, moving dust cloud out of which suddenly appeared an automobile. It was the first car the eight-year-old boy had ever seen and he started running after it.

It was an early edition Model T Ford, and many years later and now Chairman of his own motor car company, Soichiro

Honda would fondly recall: "It leaked oil, I got down on my hands and knees to smell it. It was like perfume".

Some years later, in September 1946, the now grown up Soichiro visited the home of a friend, Kenzaburo Inuka. There, by chance, he came upon a small engine which had been originally designed for a No. 6 wireless radio used by the former Imperial Army. Soichiro thought he could see another completely different use for it.

He immediately set to work on a prototype for a motorised bicycle. He took a Japanese-style hot water bottle and used it as the fuel tank. Initially he attached the engine to the front of the bicycle, but following numerous blow-outs of the front tyres, he remodelled using a more conventional engine layout with a V belt driving the rear wheel.

Among his first test riders for this new improved machine was a woman, but not just any woman. No, Honda asked his wife, Sachi to try the machine.

She recalls: *"'I've made one of these, so you try riding it.' That was what my husband said when he brought one of his machines to the house.*

"Later, he claimed that he made it because he couldn't stand to watch me working so hard at pedalling my bicycle when I went off looking for food to buy, but that was just a story he made up afterward to make it sound better – although that might have been a little part of it.

"Mainly, though, I think he really wanted to know whether a

woman could handle his bike. I was his guinea pig. He made me drive all over the main streets that were crowded with people, so I wore my best monpe [baggy trousers worn by farm women and female labourers] *when I took the bike."*

When she returned she had a bone to pick with him, though it wasn't about being used as a guinea pig but rather it was about the performance of the bike.

"After riding around for a good while, I went back to the house and my best monpe had gotten all covered with oil. I told him, this is no good. Your customers will come back and scold you.

"His usual response was, 'Oh, be quiet. Don't fuss about it.' But instead, this time he said, 'Hmm, maybe so.'

"He was unusually submissive about it."

And the reason for that submissiveness was that Honda was already thinking about how to find and solve the problem.

Honda identified that the reason for the soiling was some of the fuel/oil mixture used to power the engine was being blown back through the carburettor.

He dismantled every engine on every one of his first batch of bikes, checked them all, reassembled them with the best carburettors he could find and then as a final touch gave them all a test ride before selling them.

It was the earliest version of today's finished vehicle delivery inspections, and a guarantee that his customers wouldn't be coming back to scold him as his wife had done.

And the moral is that early prototyping can identify early problems. How soon in your innovation process do you develop real prototypes?

45 THE LONELY SMOKER

In the dark, in the rain, a lone man walks purposefully along the Embankment in London. He is dressed in a light coloured raincoat with its collar turned up and is wearing a dark trilby pulled down over his eyes.

We can't make out his face as he walks in and out of the pools of white that are cast by the streetlights. He stops in the shadows and pulls out a packet of cigarettes. As he lights one, we catch a glimpse of his handsome face. He takes a puff and moves on.

As the camera pans back, a voiceover speaks: "You're never alone with a Strand". The line is superimposed onto the screen and the commercial ends. This commercial for Strand cigarettes didn't run for long on British television, yet it is one of the most famous commercials of all time.

Indeed, in a *Sunday Times* article about the best commercials in the world, the author Fey Weldon, who worked for many years in advertising, cited it as her personal all-time favourite.

However, its fame isn't down to its success but rather to its failure. The campaign was a complete disaster.

It had set out to build on the success of *The Third Man* and other, similar, Cold War thrillers. Its aim was to create an image of mystery, intrigue and quiet self-confidence for the brand that potential users would aspire to and want to be associated with.

Instead, people thought it looked like a brand for losers – loners with no friends who were forced to walk the street at night.

And the moral is that what people hear isn't always what you say. What are people really hearing when you speak to them?

46 THE LITTLE CAR'S CONTRIBUTION TO LOW-COST FURNITURE

If you visit the IKEA website you can read all about its aims.

"At IKEA our vision is to create a better everyday life for the many people. Our business idea supports this vision by offering a wide range of well-designed, functional home furnishing products at prices so low that as many people as possible will be able to afford them."

Low prices are a cornerstone of the IKEA concept, as it is the low prices that make its well-designed, functional home furnishings so accessible "to the many people". While numerous means are used to keep the costs low, perhaps one of the most important is all down to the size of one of the first showroom employee's car.

The story, however, begins in 1943, when with a gift from his father, Ingvar Kampard established his business, using his initials, and those of the name of the farm on which he was born, Elmtaryd, and the village nearby, Agunnaryd, to create an acronym that is the now a world famous brand name.

Ingvar went door to door, selling a wide range of products from pens and wallets to watches and nylon stockings, but he was so successful that soon he couldn't do all the individual sales calls. He had to change his business model and began advertising in local newspapers, operating a makeshift mail-order service. He used the local milk van to deliver products to the nearby train station. By 1945, he had developed a rudimentary catalogue.

Locally manufactured furniture first showed up in the IKEA product range in 1947 and was so well received that by 1951 Ingvar began to focus solely on furniture, and discontinued all the other products in his catalogue.

In 1953, and in response to increasing competition, the first IKEA furniture showroom opened in the village of Älmhult. This same competition caused other furniture stores and manufacturers to put pressure on suppliers to boycott IKEA which led to the critical decision to design its own furniture beginning in 1955. It was not long after this that the fateful event happened.

One of the first workers at the storeroom purchased one of IKEA's Lövet tables. But that night as he prepared to take it home he discovered that it was too big to fit in the back of his little car. Ultimately the worker removed the legs from the table so that it would fit into his car and wouldn't get damaged during the worker's journey.

Word got round about the event and it started Ingvar and his team thinking about creating furniture that was specifically designed to be flat-packed.

In 1956, IKEA began testing the concept of flat-packs and its potential to reduce costs through reduced transportation expenses, lower storage space requirements, less transportation damage and a reduction in labour costs.

The IKEA Lövet table became the first flat-packed IKEA product and flat-packing and self-assembly become integral parts of the IKEA business concept.

And the moral is that necessity can be the mother of invention. Should you take a fresh look at some of the challenges facing you and your brand?

47 THE GLUE THAT WOULDN'T STICK

Dr. Spencer Silver was a 3M research scientist charged with developing super-strong glue for use on one of its range of adhesive tapes. He successfully developed a new adhesive, but rather than being super-strong, it was super-weak!

His new adhesive formed itself into small spheres, each with a diameter of just a paper's width. While each sphere was individually sticky, they only made intermittent contact, so when coated on to tape backing they didn't stick strongly. In fact, they could be peeled off easily.

While it was clear that Silver had discovered a most unusual new adhesive, it wasn't until four years later that a practical use was found for it, and another six years before it came to market.

The man credited with finding the killer application for the glue was a 3M new product development researcher named Arthur Fry. Fry regularly sang in his church choir and used scraps of paper as markers to keep his place in his hymnal, but was frustrated that they kept falling out.

Fry had heard about Dr. Silver's discovery while attending an internal 3M seminar, in which the scientist had espoused the virtue of the discovery in which he'd never lost faith. It was Fry who came up with the concept that the glue could be used to create a novel sort of bookmark: one that would keep its place and not fall out, but which could be removed without marking or damaging the paper to which it had been stuck. The 3M Post-it Note was born.

Its path to market still wasn't smooth: sceptics within the organization had to be persuaded and a new and complex production system had to be devised. But as Fry himself said, this difficulty was a blessing in disguise; "If it was easy then anyone could do it".

The Post-it Note was finally launched in 1980 and in 1981 was named 3M's Outstanding New Product. Fry's contribution to the business was honoured in 1986 when he was made a 3M corporate scientist. His and Dr. Silver's concept is still one of the most popular office products available.

And the moral is that not all innovations start with a consumer insight. What technologies do you have that could offer new benefits for your customers?

48 THE 5,000 FAILURES

James Dyson likes to do things "wrong".

While vacuuming his home, he became frustrated with the lousy suction of his vacuum cleaner. The bag and filter clogged too quickly, reducing the suction power to a point where he thought it hardly worked at all. Dyson decided enough was enough and he had to do something about it.

Over 15 years, he built 5,126 prototypes before he found the one that worked to his satisfaction. What took him so long? His answer would be that it took him ages to think of "wrong-doing".

He explains: *"When I was doing my vacuum cleaner, I started out trying a conventionally shaped cyclone, the kind you see in textbooks. But we couldn't separate the carpet fluff and dog hairs and strands of cotton in those cyclones. It formed a ball inside the cleaner or shot out the exit and got into the motor. I tried all sorts of shapes. Nothing worked.*

"So then I thought I'd try the wrong shape, the opposite of conical. And it worked. It was wrong-doing rather than wrong-thinking. That's not easy, because we're all taught to do things the right way."

Dyson's inspiration was a sawmill that was near to where he worked. They used a cyclone to expel waste – a 30-foot or 9.1-metre high cone that spun dust out of the air using centrifugal force. He reasoned that a vacuum cleaner that could separate dust by cyclonic action and spin it out of the airstream would eliminate the need for both bag and filter, and so of course these couldn't clog. His first production version of a dual cyclone vacuum cleaner featuring constant suction was the DC01, and it sold for £200.

Market research showed that people wouldn't be happy with a transparent container for the dust, but Dyson and his team decided on more "wrong-doing" and made a transparent container anyway. It turned out to be a distinctive, popular and enduring feature.

The DC01 became the biggest selling vacuum cleaner in the UK in just 18 months.

And the moral is that sometimes it pays to think the unthinkable and do things "wrong". Could you do something better by doing it wrong?

49 THE BATS, THE PRINCE AND THE SICK NOTE

Don Facundo Bacardi Masso was neither batty nor sick but his success and the story of Bacardi are linked to both a colony of bats and a sick note sent to him by a Queen.

Born in Spain in October 1814, Don Facundo moved to Santiago in Cuba when he was 15. There, he worked as a wine merchant and unusually for the time thought that there was a real future in rum. Most of his peers thought that the spirit was far too rough to be good for anything other than selling to the pirates who frequented the port.

Don Facundo began experimenting with making his own rum and finally found what he was looking for: a new process that incorporated a special charcoal filtration stage. It not only removed impurities but produced rum that was smoother and mellower.

He purchased a small, local, disused distillery to begin production, but on taking possession, he discovered that there were large numbers of bats living in the rafters. Instead of getting rid of the bats, he decided to let them stay; in fact, he decided to use them as an icon for the brand.

To the Cuban people bats are a sign of good health, good fortune and family unity. As his wife, Doria Amalia, pointed out, there was a very high rate of illiteracy in Cuba in the 19th Century and a new product needed a memorable logo; a visual trademark which would be easy for people to recognize.

Besides the bat, another symbol is seen on every bottle of Bacardi. It is the Spanish Royal coat of arms and it was added after Bacardi came to the aid of Queen Maria Cristina – or rather, to the aid of her son, Prince Alfonso XIII.

In 1892, the young Prince Alfonso was taken sick with a severe case of the grippe. Nothing seemed to improve his health until a royal physician who had recently returned from Cuba suggested Don Facundo's rum. That evening, for the first time in days, the Prince fell into an easy and peaceful sleep and by morning the fever was broken. The Prince was on the mend.

Royal "sick notes" were duly written to say thank you to Bacardi for producing a drink that had saved "His Majesty's life". In addition, the title of "Purveyors to the Royal Household" on Bacardi, which not only added the coat of arms to the bottle but became known as "El rey de los rones, el ron de los reyes" ("The king of rums, the rum of Kings").

And the moral is that a picture or indeed an icon can be worth more than words. Could you be making more of the images and icons linked to your brands?

50 THE DEAR JAMES LETTER

On 1 September 2012 a young boy named James wrote a letter to Lego...

LEGO Systems, Inc.
555 Taylor Road
P.O. Box 1600
Enfield, CT 06083-1600
USA

LEGO Group Headquarters
East Europe, SNG countries, the Baltic States and the Balkans

LEGO Trading A/S
DK-7190 Billund
Denmark

Dear Sirs,

My name is James Groccia and I am ten years old. I have been playing with many Lego sets and products since I was about four years old. I have brick sets, Hero Factory, Creationary, Lunar Limo and more. I participate in a Lego Playgroup to help with my Social Skills (I have Asperger's Syndrome) and I love playing with Legos at home (I play with them every day).

A couple of years ago, I saw The Emerald Night Train set (K10194) and fell in love with it. I wanted it right away, but my parents said I had to save the money to get it. For two years I kept all the money I got for birthday and holiday gifts, some of my allowance and some money I got for participating in a research project. At last, a couple of months ago I had my $100 and was ready to buy the Lego set of my dreams!

My mom started looking for it online and could not find any. We checked the Lego store in our area and they didn't have it either. I was completely crushed. You've stopped making it! It seems the only way to get one now is to pay $250 on Amazon or ebay, since now it is considered collectible.

I got another Lego set, thinking I could forget about the Emerald Night, but every time I see it anywhere online I get very sad and disappointed. I still want the Emerald Night so badly, but there are none to be found.

Do you have any at your corporate headquarters? Perhaps I could get one that way? If you have any other ideas, I would be happy to hear them. I have never wanted a Lego set so badly ever in my life!

Your most loyal Lego fan,
James G. Groccia

On 13 September he received this reply...

Dear James,

Thanks for your interest in our products.

James, I'm afraid that we no longer make the Emerald Night. I understand how upsetting this news can be. I realize that you saved up your money to purchase it. I do apologize for any disappointment this news may have caused you.

The toy store shelves aren't big enough to hold everything, so sometimes we have to stop making a few of the older sets. Meanwhile, we have a team of experts in Denmark whose job it is to invent LEGO® toys every year. They spend their time trying to create new and fun toys for children of all ages.

You never know though, some of the old favourites sometimes make a comeback, so keep a look out! The best way to track down discontinued LEGO sets or individual pieces is to check the following secondary market websites: http://www.bricklink.com/ and htto://www.peequestion surbron.com

Please note that these websites are not affiliated with the LEGO Group.

I hope one of our many new LEGO toys will inspire the LEGO fans in your home. To take a look through the hundreds of sets and toys go to www.LEGOshop.com and remember to keep an eye on the "Exclusives and Hard to Find" section, which includes classic and collectible sets!

Thanks again for contacting us. We are always pleased to receive feedback from LEGO fans! If you could take a moment to complete a four-question survey, it will help us make sure we are providing the best customer service to you.

Sincerely,
Thomas
LEGO Direct Consumer Services

But then, about a month later, on 17 October, a box arrived at James' house along with another letter:

Dear James,

We are always thrilled to hear from our LEGO fans! You truly have a passion and joy for LEGO. I am amazed at how many sets you have at only ten years old! I am a very big LEGO fan myself and enjoy some of the same sets you do. We received your letter here in Consumer Services and were very touched by your determination.

The Emerald Night Train is a wonderful set, so we can understand why it is your dream to own it. I commend your willpower and patience to save money for over two years just to purchase this set. It is very evident that no other set could make you happier. We can understand how disappointing it must have been to find it had been discontinued. Due to your passion for LEGO and your heart-warming letter, we knew we had to go above and beyond to help make this a reality.

We have located an Emerald Night Train for you, James, and included it in this package! I am sure you will enjoy building it and cherish your time playing with the train. We are excited to know that we could help make this dream come true for you! Now there will be no more sadness or disappointment when you think about it ... just happiness!

We hope you will continue to love to build and create with LEGO. Fans like you are why we are so lucky as a company. Who knows, maybe you will be working for The LEGO Group one day! You certainly have the heart and passion for our bricks to do so! Happy building, James![4]

Sincerely,
Megan
Consumer Services Advisor

And the moral is that little gestures can have a big impact. What are the little gestures you could and perhaps should be making?

51 IF AT FIRST YOU DON'T SUCCEED, CHEW AND CHEW AGAIN

What Milton S. Hershey lacked in formal education, he more than made up for in perseverance.

Born in 1857 in rural Pennsylvania, Milton quickly learnt that there was always work to be done. With his work on the family farm and time spent looking after his mother while his father was away for long periods, Milton had a

[4] If you still aren't moved, then watch the video on YouTube: "Why LEGO is the BEST Company in the World" http://www.youtube.com/watch?v=4xGU-5KVS_g

very limited education. He had no schooling after the fourth grade, but grew up with a belief in the value of hard work.

As a teenager, he took a four-year apprenticeship with a candy maker in Lancaster, Pennsylvania and in 1876 attempted to start his own candy business. Despite six years of hard work, it failed.

So he dusted himself down and moved to Denver where he found work with a confectioner who taught him how to make caramels using fresh milk. He used his knowledge to start a second candy business in New York City, which was also ultimately unsuccessful.

Returning to Lancaster in 1886, Hershey wasn't ready to give up. He established the Lancaster Caramel Company, which quickly became an outstanding success. Soon the company was shipping its caramels all over the US and Europe, employing 1,400 people.

Milton was not done yet. At the 1893 World's Columbian Exposition in Chicago, he became fascinated with the art of chocolate making. He purchased some German machinery at the exposition, had it shipped to Lancaster and began producing chocolate coatings for his caramels. Aware of the growing demand for chocolate, he also started the Hershey Chocolate Company.

It took time and patience before success arrived. Most milk chocolate at the time was produced by a process that was kept a closely guarded secret by the Swiss. After a number of years and through repeated trial and error, however, Milton finally hit upon the right formula of milk, sugar and cocoa. It enabled him to realize his dream of cost-effectively mass-producing milk chocolate candy and turned what had once been a luxury for the rich into an enjoyment that anyone could afford – the Hershey bar.

And the moral is that if at first you don't succeed, try and try again. Are you in danger of giving up on something too soon?

52 ANY COLOUR AS LONG AS IT IS ARMY GREEN

In 1945 in the newly renamed city of Wolfsberg, a number of dusty, disused and seemingly unwanted car parts lay in the basement of a factory bombed by the British Royal Air Force. There they lay until Colonel Charles Radclyffe and Major Ivan Hirst of the British Royal Electrical & Mechanical Engineers came across them and saw what others had missed: a short-term solution to the British military's need for economically produced vehicles, and a longer-term potential to help get Germany back on its feet.

The parts were all that was left of the "People's Car", first produced in 1933 and part of Hitler's "economic miracle". Thousands of these cheap, utilitarian cars had been built at the factory prior to its conversion to the production of Luftwaffe aircraft.

Despite apparent severe damage to the factory, Major Hirst

quickly realized its potential. Having cleared some debris from the generating plant building, Hirst discovered that some of the rubble had been put there to disguise the fact that it was still operational.

The original blueprints for the car had been destroyed in the Allied bombings, leaving Major Hirst and Colonel Radclyffe to painstakingly reconstruct them from the remaining parts. They produced two folios of new technical drawings, each containing 18 tabbed sections detailing the parts and specifications of what was to go on to become one of the iconic automobiles of all time.

Production restarted in 1946 with the order for 20,000 Type 1 "Beetles" for the British Army – in, to paraphrase Henry Ford, any colour so long as it was army green.

Raw materials were in short supply and it was a constant struggle to source steel, glass and tyres. Malnutrition amongst factory workers was a key problem as food was also in short supply, so the lawns next to the factory were turned into vegetable gardens to grow extra food. Despite all this, by March 1946 the one thousandth Beetle had been produced.

In May 1949, Volkswagenwerk AG was formed and in October the Volkswagen factory was officially handed back to the Germans under the leadership of Heinz Nordhoff.

At the end of 1951, Major Hirst[5] was demobbed and returned

5 Ivan Hirst died on 10 March 2000 aged 84. There is still a street near the original VW factory that was named after him in appreciation of the work he did to help put Germany on the road to recovery: Major-Hirst-Straße, Wolfsburg.

to civilian life in England. The Beetle, the Bug (as it's known in the USA), the Kaefer (as it's known in Germany) went from strength to strength.

And the moral is (with a nod to another iconic car – Chitty Chitty Bang Bang) that sometimes from the ashes of disaster grow the roses of success. How can you use a past failure to drive future success?

53 A VERY SPECIAL BREW

Sir Winston Leonard Spencer-Churchill was given many prizes and awards in his lifetime; he is the only British Prime Minister to have received the Nobel Prize in Literature and was the first person to be made an Honorary Citizen of the United States.

To honour Churchill's contribution to Denmark and the Danish people, Carlsberg decided to create a new beer, commemorating his visit to Copenhagen in 1950. The move followed the Danish tradition of producing a new beer to celebrate outstanding events, such as a European coronation or birth of a royal baby.

Carlsberg knew from its research that Churchill's favourite drink wasn't actually beer but cognac. Rather than being put off by this fact, it used it for inspiration: the brewer created a 9% lager, stronger than normal, with cognac flavours among its tasting notes. Carlsberg called the new beer "V-øllet", literally "V-Beer", echoing VE and VJ day.

When Churchill returned to Britain, Carlsberg sent two crates of the beer to his London address. Clearly a man of judgment and taste and of course a skilled politician and diplomat, Churchill sent a letter to the brewery in which he thanked it for what he called "Commemoration Lager".

In the years to follow, the drink was renamed "Påskebryg" ("Easter Brew"), and then replaced by a weaker beer named ("Carls Påske"). In the late 1950s, Carlsberg decided it would try selling the beer in Britain and production was started in Northampton. It was given yet another name, but this time the name would stick: "Carlsberg Special Brew".[6]

And the moral is that products may need to be evolved or repositioned to find their most successful niche. Have all your products or services found their optimum position?

---

6 The author Kingsley Amis was also a big fan of Special Brew and used to mix it, half and half, with ordinary Carlsberg in a large tankard. No other drink, he said, has the same ability "to create goodwill".

In 1980, a ska band called Bad Manners had a huge hit with a single entitled *Special Brew*, which stayed in the UK charts for 13 weeks: *"I don't care, when they stare at the way I'm always with you. We're a pair; it's not fair when they say we're a special brew."*

At 9% alcohol, Special Brew is part of a group of strong lagers that are now termed "super-strength" in the UK and "malt liquors" in the US. Unfortunately its strength means that it is associated with street alcoholics and this has led the brand to acquiring an unsavoury reputation and a host of other names including "tramp juice".

54 THE WHITE KNIGHT AND THE CHOC ICE

When Sir Richard Branson decided in 1984 to use the money he had received for the sale of Virgin Records to launch a lower-cost transatlantic airline, many commentators were surprised. It had been only two years since Sir Freddie Laker's Skytrain outfit had gone out of business.

At launch, however, it quickly became apparent that, even if he hadn't done any formal market research, Branson's own experiences had provided him with real insights into the needs of other flyers.

Sir Richard put himself in the position of consumer champion, becoming their white knight and offering something that he believed they wanted but weren't getting from existing airlines.

When Virgin Atlantic started flying, one of the most obvious differences in their planes was that there weren't just a few large screens in each cabin compartment; there was a screen on the back of every seat. Sir Richard explained that he had always hated the fact that travellers were offered a movie on their flight but could rarely see what was being shown. Movies on planes were generally a disagreeable event as people went up and down to stretch their legs or go to the toilet.

Screens on the back of each seat meant that everyone had a personal screen. Not only did this mean that passengers could watch the movie, but Virgin also included a video games package in case they would prefer to play games.

To cap it all, halfway through the movie the cabin crew came round with choc ices. Well, if you go to the movies you want an ice-cream, don't you?

And the moral is that it pays to put yourself in your customers' shoes. When did you last "mystery shop" your own brand?

55 A TIRED OLD STORY?

A middle-aged man is wheeling a tyre (or as this story takes place in America, it is probably fairer to say a "tire") up and down outside a Nordstrom store in Fairbanks, Alaska. He keeps stopping and peering in through the window. He looks a bit confused. Soon he starts to walk up and down again.

After a few minutes, he enters into the Nordstrom store and wheels the tire up to one of the cash desks. There the clerk offers a bright "Good morning, can I help you?"

Completely unbeknownst to the clerk, standing in the background are John Nordstrom, a member of the store's founding family, and the store manager. They are both watching with interest.

"I hope so," says the man, a little bit embarrassed. "I bought this tire in this store, never got round to fitting it and don't need it anymore. I was hoping to return it."

Now this is a Nordstrom store, part of a chain of department stores that sell a wide range of men and ladies fashion, but not automotive products, and certainly not tires. Despite this the clerk asks: "Do you have a receipt?"

"I'm afraid not," answers the man.

"Well, can you remember how much it cost?"

"I think it was about $25."

"Okay," says the clerk and opens up his till. He takes out $25 and hands it over to the man, who smiles, thanks the clerk and leaves the store.

John Nordstrom and the store manager look at each other, walk straight over to the clerk and say ... "Well done".

Now being praised by your senior management for giving a refund on a product that your company doesn't even sell may seem a little strange, but there is a little more to the story, and a lot more to Nordstrom's approach to customer service.

The "little more" to the story is that the man may have been confused because that particular Nordstrom store was one of three stores that had previously been owned and run by NCC (Northern Commercial Company) and were sold to

Nordstrom. NCC operated department stores, but it also operated auto-dealerships and tire centres, so the man may well have bought the tire from it.

The "lot more" is that since it began in 1901, Nordstrom has prided itself on its customer service and has become almost synonymous with service. It has a liberal, no-quibble returns policy. Those looking to make a return are not challenged to produce receipts for goods that are clearly Nordstrom stock. Sales staff are known to personally deliver special orders to customers' homes. They are universally knowledgeable and courteous. They genuinely seem to want to help customers.

And behind this sits one of the most interesting employee handbooks in the world.

It reads (in its entirety)...

EMPLOYEE HANDBOOK

Welcome to Nordstrom. We're glad you're here.

Our number one goal is to provide outstanding customer service. Set both your personal and professional goals high. We have great confidence in your ability to achieve them, so our employee handbook is very simple. We have only one rule...

OUR ONE RULE
Use good judgement in all situations.
Please feel free to ask your department manager, store manager or Human Resources officer any question at any time.

And that's it.[7]

And the moral is that empowering employees can power your brand. Do you trust your staff to always do the right thing?

56 THE 13-TON WRISTWATCH

Swiss watches have long been associated with luxury and craftsmanship. They have a reputation for being beautiful, beautifully made and very expensive, but by the 1980s Swiss watches were suffering from heavy competition from inexpensive Asian watches. The new quartz technology had revolutionized watchmaking. A once proud industry employing nearly 90,000 in the late 1960s had seen that figure drop to less than 35,000.

In this post-quartz watch world, the Swiss watch industry desperately needed to broaden its appeal and the Swatch brand was created to lead the way.

[7] The tire story is a well-known tale and part of Nordstrom's folklore. There is, however, much debate as to whether or not it is true. There are other versions of it but all centre on the acceptance of tires that clearly Nordstrom never sold but still took back. However, what I can personally confirm is true is the existence of the handbook and its exact contents. I wrote to Nordstrom in 2012 and asked if the handbook which I had first heard about many years ago still existed.

A short time later I received a personal letter back from Jamie Nordstrom, President, Nordstrom Direct, in which he says the employee handbook, which is in fact an A5 card, "continues to be a part of our culture. Our new employees receive the card on the first day of training". He kindly enclosed a copy of the card. It still makes me smile when I compare it with other employee handbooks I have seen.

To succeed, however, Swatch would need to challenge existing perceptions of Swiss watches. It would be a big job, and the answer – at least in Germany – came in the form of a big statement: a gigantic, fully working, 13-ton, 162-metre high, bright orange Swatch that was suspended on the tallest building in Frankfurt, the commercial capital of Germany. Oh yes and the building just happened to be the headquarters of one of Germany leading financial institutions – the Commerzbank.

On the watch was printed three things: "Swatch" (the brand name), "Swiss" (its origins) and its price "DM60" (the surprise).

"It was a big provocation to hang a watch from a huge grim skyscraper. And it was funny, fanciful, a joke – joy of life. Believe me when we took it down everyone we wanted to reach had received our message," said Nicolas Hayek, the head of SMH.

The message everyone received was that here was a Swiss watch, which had all the heritage of local craftsmanship, but was a brand with a sense of humour and available at a price not previously associated with Swiss quality.

Behind this great publicity stunt was someone who came up with the idea and a team that had the skill to build the giant watch, but there was another less obvious team who needed all their ingenuity to sell the idea to Commerzbank. Without the agreement of the bank, Frankfurt would never have got its own equivalent of London's Big Ben.

What this last team did was to put themselves in the shoes

of the President of the Commerzbank and identify what they thought were the main problems he might have with the concept, so that they could prepare solutions in advance.

While they recognized that there would be many little details they would need to address, the real and major concerns would be two-fold: the impact on the reputation of the Commerzbank brand and the practicalities of making it happen.

To address the first issue, the team commissioned some original research – not amongst potential Swatch customers but amongst Commerzbank customers. Helpfully, the findings showed that rather than seeing the stunt negatively, Commerzbank customers liked the idea of the bank showing its human face through its involvement in such a bold act.

Next, the team approached the local civic authorities and got their buy-in in the form of a written approval of the scheme.

With these two trump cards, the team was finally ready to go and meet the President of the Commerzbank. By all accounts, he did raise his concerns but was impressed by the Swatch's team planning, and they came away with his approval to proceed. The watch was mounted on the side of the bank in 1984.[8]

And the moral is that it pays to have solutions to future problems ready in advance. Are you really thinking ahead about the challenges you may face?

---

[8] The watch is in the *Guinness Book of World Records* as the world's largest wristwatch. If you want to see the pictures they are still available on the Commerzbank website: https://www.commerzbank.com/en/hauptnavigation/presse/bilddaten/commerzbank_s_past/commerzbank_s_past_1.html

57 THE ROLLS ROYCE AND THE KETTLE

JCB (or more formally J.C. Bamford Excavators Limited) was founded by Joseph Cyril Bamford in October 1945 in Uttoxeter, Staffordshire, England.

After the war, Bamford initially worked for English Electric developing electric welding equipment. A short return stint with the family firm proved unsuccessful, and his Uncle Henry released him, saying he thought Joe had "little future ahead of him".

So in October 1945 Bamford rented a small lock-up garage for 30 shillings (£1.50) a week. In it, using a welding set which he bought second-hand for £1 from English Electric, he made his first vehicle: a tipping trailer. It was made from war-surplus Jeep axles and steel sheeting that had been part of air-raid shelters, amongst other things.

On the day his son Anthony was born, Joe sold the trailer at a nearby market for £45 (plus a part-exchanged farm cart) and at once made another trailer. It was the beginning of an on-going success.

Part of Bamford's success was down to the fact that he was different from many engineers; he had an instinct for customer service and innovation. Bamford personally demanded to know daily from his staff how many "JCB Yellow" vehicles were off the road awaiting spares. Bamford created an image that JCBs were there to work, and if an owner-operator's machine was down, then he wanted to know about it.

He also knew that customers liked the personal touch and so even in his 60s he would often accompany a new vehicle as it was delivered, doing so in his Rolls-Royce with its distinctive JCB1 number plate. "They like to see a British manufacturer in a Rolls-Royce, it gives distributers confidence," he would say.

One day he accompanied Head Demonstrator, John Wheeldon, a long-term colleague and friend, as he delivered a new machine to a client in Derbyshire. John Wheeldon went through a full display of all the exciting features and the highly impressed client said, "This does everything but make the tea!"

Bamford went straight home and tweaked the cab's design that very night – so that since then, for nearly 50 years, every JCB has had a kettle and a power socket on board. Some of the latest ones have actually got coffee machines...[9]

Bamford continued to accompany the delivery of new vehicles and would personally carry the kettle separately in his Rolls so he could formally present it to the new owners

And the moral is that even when you think you have thought of everything, there is always room for improvement. What are you doing to make your offer even better?

---

[9] JCB has a unique place in popular culture:
- In 1958 the singer Lenny Green had a song called *JCB and Me*.
- In the UK version of the *Teletubbies*, one of the live-action visual five-minute segments featured number counting involving vehicles in lines. A row of JCBs are seen in line, their hydraulics operated as if they are "dancing".
- The Lego Technic range featured a scale-model of the JCB backhoe (Set 8862), complete with working hydraulics systems (simulated using pneumatics) and many other features of the original.
- In series 9 of *Top Gear*, Jeremy Clarkson bought a JCB Fastrac 8250 and he, James May and Richard Hammond all had to reverse their vehicles around the *Top Gear* car park.

58 RED STAR AT NIGHT, BREWERS DELIGHT?

A five-pointed and red (filled) star is an important ideological and religious symbol. It has been used as a state emblem, on flags and on monuments. It is also used frequently as a symbol of communism.

Just how the star came to be associated with communism and what it stands for is a matter of long-standing debate, but there are three widespread explanations.

The simplest is that the five points represent the five fingers of a worker's hand.

A second explanation suggests that the origin lies in an encounter between Leon Trotsky and Nikolai Krylenko. Krylenko was a Russian Bolshevik and was to become People's Commissar for Justice and Prosecutor General of the Russian Soviet Federated Socialist Republic. At their meeting, Krylenko was wearing a green-star lapel badge. Trotsky enquired about its meaning; he was told that each arm of the star represented one of the five traditional continents. Hearing this, Trotsky decided a similar red star should be worn by soldiers of the Red Army.

The third explanation is linked with the Russian civil war and the end of World War I. The story runs that in 1917 the Russian troops, fleeing from the Austrian and German fronts, found themselves in Moscow. To distinguish local Moscow garrison troops from this influx of retreating soldiers, officers gave out tin stars to members of the garrison

Moscow, to be worn on their hats. When those troops later joined the Red Army and the Bolsheviks, it is said that they painted the tin stars red, the colour of socialism.

Long before the red star was connected with communism, however, it was an icon for Heineken.[10] Here, the story of its origins becomes even more complicated, with four different explanations for its use now in circulation.

The first is that the red star was a symbol of European brewers in the Middle Ages, who believed it held mystical powers to protect their brew. Heineken adopted it because of this long association with brewing, and its suggestion of a quality beer.

Again coming from the Middle Ages, the second possible explanation is that four points of the star represent the four "classical elements" of earth, fire, water and wind, while the fifth is "the unknown", an element that brewers couldn't control.

A third explanation is that the position of a star on the front door of the brewery indicated a particular stage of the brewing process. Over time, the symbol became associated with the beer and not the brewing process.

The final explanation – and a strong favourite when viewed from a branding perspective – is that the five points represent the five ingredients that make Heineken so special. These are the traditional four natural ingredients found in all beers

[10] During the height of the Cold War period, the original design of the Heineken star was altered to avoid too direct an association with communism. It was changed to a white star with a red outline, but has since been changed back to the original full red star. Heineken today say that for it, the red star's principle association is a festive, warm and cheerful mood.

(malt, yeast, hops and water) and a fifth special one – the magic of the Heineken brewers.

And the moral is that a little magic, a little mystery can add to a brand's appeal. Where is the magic in your brand?

59 THE NO-NEWS GOOD NEWS

The world's very first underground route opened on 9 January 1863. It ran for just six kilometers (nearly four miles) between Paddington (Bishop's Road) and Farringdon Street in London.

Nowadays, there are 11 lines and over 250 stations, but despite being the first of its kind, London Underground – or as it is more commonly known, the Tube - had a very poor reputation for many years.

Trains were crammed, stations were shabby and strikes were felt to be all too regular for passengers' liking. The Northern line was widely known as "the misery line".

From the end of the 1980s things began to change, however. Many commentators point to three key factors that led to the change.

The first was the horror of the 1987 King's Cross fire, in which 31 people died. It led to the Fennell Report and the realization that years of under-investment had been at the heart of the disaster.

The second came after the Labour party was elected in 1997, when then-chancellor Gordon Brown committed himself to funding the Underground through a Public-Private Partnership.

The third factor was that the Tube became a regular and important focus in the political battle to become Mayor of London. Nationally, railways have rarely if ever been a major electoral issue, but transport is the Mayor of London's prime responsibility and the Underground is the most crucial – because most utilized – part of that.

All of this attention began to pay off.

In 1982, fewer than 2 million people a day had been using the Underground but by 2002 figures were up to more than 3.5 million. There were upgrades on the Victoria and Metropolitan lines; the new electronic Oyster card made payments easier and faster; and many stations had been refurbished.

Yet despite all the improvements, satisfaction ratings were still poor, and users' perceptions more negative than had been hoped.

So the situation remained until a fourth and almost unnoticed change came into play: the "no news, good news" announcements.

For many years, only two types of announcements were ever heard on the tube. The first were those for specific platforms: "The next train is approaching"; "This train is all stations to High Barnet"; and the more famous "Stand clear of the doors" and "Mind the gap".

The other type of announcement was made station-wide, reporting problems on the network: "Severe delays on the Victoria line"; "Please check for delays at the weekend"; "No trains on the Circle line due to planned engineering works"; "Finchley Road station is closed"; "The 8.36 has been cancelled due to lack of drivers."...Bad news announcements.

It was a consultant to London Underground who recognized that these messages were a problem. It wasn't that London Underground shouldn't be making this type of announcement; in fact, best practice in customer service suggests businesses should admit and communicate problems. No, the real problem was that all these bad news announcements weren't offset with any good news.

The solution the consultant suggested was novel: to introduce "no news" announcements. He suggested London Underground give regular service updates even when there was nothing new to say; when everything was normal.

What these no-news announcements did was to demonstrate the reality of the situation; namely that for much of the time there really was no news, simply, "a good service operating on all London Underground lines". In London Underground's case, no news was in fact good news and deserved to be told.

Nowadays the London Underground network carries more than 1 billion passengers a year. That's over 3 and a half million journeys made each day, and most passengers hear regular updates on the network. Of course there are still some problems, but nowadays a traveller on the Tube will regularly hear that "there is a good service operating on all

London Underground Lines".

By 2009, London Underground had some real news to announce – and that news was good. Passenger satisfaction ratings hit a new high with average scores reaching 79 out of 100 and the Tube had just been named Best Metro in Europe, beating off stiff competition from Paris, Madrid, Berlin and Copenhagen.

And the moral is that nothing bad happening can sometimes be as good as something good happening. What performances are you taking for granted?

60 FROM THE ISLE OF SKY TO BUCKINGHAM PALACE, A 171-YEAR JOURNEY

The Battle of Culloden (or in Gaelic, Blàr Chùil Lodair) was the final confrontation of the Jacobite Rising. On 16 April 1746, the Jacobite forces of Prince Charles Edward Stuart, more commonly known as Bonnie Prince Charlie, fought the loyalist troops commanded by William Augustus, Duke of Cumberland, near Inverness in the Scottish Highlands.

The conflict was the last pitched battle fought on British soil, but its other claim to fame is that it is the first stage on the journey of one of the world's most famous liqueur brand. It was a journey that would take 171 years for the drink to travel from the Isle of Skye to Buckingham Palace, from one royal household to another.

Having lost the battle, Bonnie Prince Charlie fled, but was pursued by the King's men across the Highlands and Islands of Western Scotland. During this flight, he was aided by many Highland Clans, amongst them was Clan MacKinnon. It was their chief, Captain John MacKinnon, who helped the Prince escape across the sea to the Isle of Skye.

There, he was given sanctuary by the Captain and in thanks for the man's bravery, the Prince gave John MacKinnon the secret recipe to his personal liqueur. It was a gift that the Clan were to treasure down the generations.

More than 100 years later, the recipe passed to John Ross of The Broadford Hotel on Skye, where he developed and improved the recipe and the drink gained its now famous brand name. It is said that upon tasting it one of these locals exclaimed that this was "the drink that satisfies", – or in Gaelic, "an dram buidheach". This was shortened to '"Drambuie" and was registered as a trademark in 1893.

Ross died young, and to pay for their children's education, his widow sold the recipe, by coincidence to a different MacKinnon family, in the early 20th Century.

In 1900 the brand's journey continued, as Malcolm MacKinnon travelled from Skye to Edinburgh to work in the wines and spirits trade. There he realized the opportunity that the liqueur offered, and in 1909 he produced the first commercial bottling for his company MacBeth & Sons. By 1914, he had acquired the recipe and trademark, and he established The Drambuie Liqueur Company.

Success soon followed and the brand travelled south to England. In 1916, Drambuie became the first liqueur to be allowed in the cellars of the House of Lords.

A year later, Buckingham Palace ordered a case for its cellars...and the brand was back in a Royal household again

And the moral is that not all innovations are overnight successes. Are you keeping faith in ideas that you believe will be slow-burn successes?

61 WHERE'S EDDIE?

"Eddie Spotting" is a cult game in the UK that boasts a fan club of more than 20,000 members. It involves identifying the distinctive green, white and red lorries that bear the gold letters of Carlisle-based road haulier Eddie Stobart Limited.

Fans, including the famous musician Jools Holland, vie with each other to spot as many company lorries as possible in the course of a single journey. For these fans – and even for some non-fans – a journey is not complete without seeing at least one of Eddie's lorries; waving to the driver and getting an acknowledging "honk" in return.

The Eddie Stobart story starts in the 1950s when Eddie (Senior) founded an agricultural contracting business. However, it was when Edward Stobart, Eddie's son, left school at 14 and joined the company that things really began to change.

Edward's first job was to find additional employment for the trucks as much of the firm's business was seasonal. Edward proved himself successful and business soon picked up, so much so that in 1975, aged just 20, Edward took the Eddie Stobart name and began to turn it into a dedicated transport company. A year later, the company moved into a new depot in Carlisle, and by 1980 the company had grown to 25 vehicles and 35 staff.

The business continued to grow and gradually it moved away from working for other hauliers to concentrate exclusively on dealing direct with manufacturers, such as Spillers and Metal Box.

Hard work, never refusing an order, and taking those orders round the clock for just-in-time delivery slots were all part of the success, but Edward believes that the brand's image was vital too:

"Transport has had a shifty image for such a long time. The average truck driver or small operator was basically a tramp. Service in the industry needed to be upgraded, so we put in standards which others are now following."

By breaking with this norm and via an extraordinary commitment to courtesy, appearance and service, Edward Stobart was to create a powerful brand for himself and change the face of road haulage in the UK.

"Image is very important in anything you do in this country. You only get one chance of making a first impression. Basically, you have got to have manners and be courteous at all times.

Drivers must look the part."

So Edward insisted that his drivers really looked the part. They were made to wear a tie and a smart green jacket and indeed, if any driver was caught not wearing a tie while on duty, he or she could face disciplinary action.

But ties were not the only thing that made Eddie Stobart drivers and their lorries stand out. Drivers had to keep their lorries, each of which was given a women's name, immaculately clean. Years later Edward explained that all along he knew *"the tie wasn't the important thing about the uniform, it was the discipline".*

"We are one of the cheapest operators because we are run efficiently and properly. Quality and standards pull the price down. Washing our trucks and insisting our drivers wear a uniform actually reduces costs. It is only silly people who say they can't afford to do that."

And looking back, another of those "silly" policies seems to have paid off too. It stated that all drivers must wave back and honk their horn in the traditional truck-driver fashion when signalled by a passer-by.

"Eddie spotters" were born, and the fan club and a host of Eddie Stobart memorabilia soon followed. Keep your eyes peeled on your next motorway trip and you too might spot one...

And the moral is that your brand image and the impressions it makes are important. How do you ensure you always project the image you want?

62 THE PARSIMONIOUS BOSS AND THE $99 REQUISITIONS

Dick (or Richard G. if you're being formal) Drew became a 3M research assistant, though this hadn't been his first, or even his second, choice of career. He had wanted to be a banjo player, had taken and dropped out of a course in engineering and so instead he ended up using his limited knowledge of chemistry to start his career at 3M

At this point in its history, 3M primarily manufactured sandpaper and other abrasives, and one of Drew's first jobs was taking samples of the company's new Wetordry waterproof sandpaper to nearby auto body shops for testing.

One morning in 1923, as he walked into one of these shops, Drew overheard the "choicest profanity I'd ever known". Another two-tone paint job had just been botched and the worker who had been working on it was furious.

Curious, Drew asked what the problem was.

Two-tone cars were all the rage in the roaring 20s, but the effect required workers to mask certain parts of the auto's body while the two types of paint were being applied. The mechanics, having nothing specifically designed for the job, used either a combination of heavy adhesive tape and butcher paper or old newspapers and library pastes or even surgical adhesive tape.

After the paint dried, workers then had to remove the tape – and more often than not as they took off the paper or the tape they peeled away part of the new paint too. All their hard work was wasted.

Now Drew had he been just a salesmen and not an innovator could perhaps have seen this as an opportunity to sell more sandpaper, but instead he realized that what the customer really needed was a tape with less aggressive adhesive.

He rashly announced that he would solve their problem, believing that 3M already had several of the elements he would need to create his new tape; sandpaper required a backing, an adhesive and an abrasive mineral. Drew's idea was simple: hold the mineral and you'll have an adhesive tape.

Drew took his idea back to the lab. He began a long and frustrating quest for the right combination of materials to create what would become the world's first tape specifically designed for masking.

Drew wrestled with the adhesive and, especially, the backing. After some time, then-President McKnight told Drew to drop the project and get back to work on improving sandpaper.

Drew agreed – for about 24 hours. Then he thought of a new way to handle the backings and went back to the lab. He threw himself into the task with renewed enthusiasm, ignoring McKnight's orders.

Drew finally hit on what he believed was the right combination of materials, and asked McKnight to approve funding for a paper-making machine needed to manufacture the new tape. McKnight considered the proposal, and refused.

Rather than give up, Drew simply applied his talent for improvisation to this problem. In his capacity as a researcher, he had authority to approve purchases of up to $100, so he began writing a flurry of $99 purchase orders.

Now with his machine installed he created a prototype which had adhesive along its edges but not in the middle. In its first trial run, it fell off the car and the frustrated auto painter growled at Drew: "Take this tape back to those Scotch bosses of yours and tell them to shove it!"

The painter had been using "Scotch" to mean "parsimonious", but Drew was struck by the nickname, and like future versions of the tape, it stuck.

After adapting the prototype by adding more adhesive, Scotch Masking Tape was finally and successfully launched.

Drew finally confessed to McKnight about how he had managed to fund the machinery he had required and perhaps not surprisingly given Masking Tape's success, McKnight didn't fire him.[11]

And the moral is that ideas aren't the only problem; executing them right is crucial too. Do you have a great idea that just needs more work?

[11] McKnight's decision not to fire Drew was to prove to be the right one when Drew went on to create a variant of his masking tape using DuPont's new cellophane as its backing. This new variant was launched on 8 September 1930 and was originally called Scotch® Brand Cellulose Tape and later renamed Scotch® Transparent Tape. In the UK it is now known as Sellotape and in the US more simply as Scotch tape.

63 THE INSANELY GREAT $50-MILLION GAMBLE

Steve Jobs will be forever intrinsically linked with the Apple brand, but his part in the story of another brand was also pivotal. It was his investment, his gamble that was to help make that brand insanely great.

"Pixar Animation Studios wouldn't exist without Steve Jobs. It's pretty remarkable to think about what he gave us. When he bought us [in 1986] he had just left Apple. He had just started to form his company NeXT and he bought our group from Lucasfilm," explains John Lasseter.

"In the beginning Pixar was a computer company. We did hardware and software. It was a very high-end computer; it was way ahead of its time, so frankly there was no market for it. It was very expensive. Steve was trying to figure out a way to sell it and market it. He had been used to the consumer computer world but this was more of a professional world."

Pixar's core product was in fact the Pixar Image Computer, a system primarily sold, when it sold at all, to government agencies and the medical community.

It was in a bid to drive sales of the Pixar Image Computer that Lasseter, the only traditionally trained Disney animator at the company, started to create short demonstration animations (such as *Luxo Jr*) to show off the device's capabilities. He premiered his creations at SIGGRAPH, the computer graphics industry's largest convention, to great fanfare.

As a result, Lasseter's animation department began producing computer-animated commercials for outside companies. Early successes included campaigns for Tropicana, Listerine, Life Savers and *Terminator 2: Judgment Day*.

But poor sales of Pixar's computers threatened to put the company out of business. In April 1990, Jobs sold Pixar's hardware division to Viacom Systems and in 1991 another 30 employees were let go. This left just the software programmers and Lasseter's animation department.

Jobs, who by this time had invested $50 million of his own money, was tempted to sell the whole company but instead choose to take a risk as he saw a different future for a new Pixar.

"Steve was always very supportive of letting us continue the animation research. He really started seeing the potential of the evolution of Pixar, from a computer company to an animation studio. And then he saw the vision of us doing a feature film with Toy Story. *He kept guiding us.*

"The only thing he ever asked for me was to make it great. The famous term he used was 'make it insanely great'. That's what he strove for us to do. Always. And he loved the fact that we were doing things that nobody else had ever done.

"Two things I remember him telling me. One was how important quality is to what we do.

"He said that 'the way that the audience feels about your brand is like a bank account – you can either make deposits or you can make withdrawals'. Deposits are of course making

something great that everyone really loves. A withdrawal is putting out something you know isn't very good but you still put your name on it. He refused to ever do that.

"That was so vital to him, how people cared about our brand and it really permeated into Pixar. There are 1,200 people at Pixar now. If you ask any one of them, 'What's the most important thing to you?' In most of Hollywood people might say, 'What's in it for me?', but at Pixar, all 1,200 people would answer number one Pixar, number two the movie you're working on and down the line, then they'd get to themselves.

"The other thing he said to me that I'll never forget was when we were working on Toy Story, *before he went back to Apple.*

"He and I would talk all the time. We became like brothers. He would stare off sometimes and just start thinking. One time he was doing this and he said, 'Back when we were making computers at Apple, the lifespan of these computers were three years, in five years you'd have a doorstop. You do your job right and these movies can last forever.'

"And in animation we have that opportunity. Name another movie from 1938 that's seen as much today as Snow White and the Seven Dwarfs. *That simple statement has kept me focused on the right thing when making our movies – the stories and the characters.*

"Steve always drove us to get to the higher level. It's great for business, right, and we've been very successful with our films. But it's because of the quality and Steve always pushed for that, quality in every way."

And the moral is that your brand is like a bank account. When are you going to make the next deposit?

64 WOULD YOU, WOULDN'T YOU?

You have a major decision to make. It's make or break time – what are you going to do?

There is a possible opportunity in the market in which you operate. If it succeeds, it could be the future of the market; if it fails, it could mean the end of your company. You have little presence in this sector of the market and in fact have experienced one or two minor failures before. No other competitor has yet achieved a major success in this area. Indeed, your main rival believes the future lies in the currently dominant sectors.

Your engineers are excited about the opportunity and technical challenges, but your sales force reports that potential clients in your main geographical markets, the US and Europe, have expressed little interest in this type of product. They seem particularly uninterested in an offering from your brand, which they see as intrinsically linked to your current market sector.

Your current, successful business has one major client, which accounts for around 80% of your business. They may just be interested, to a relatively small extent, in a version of the product you are developing. If they buy in, it will help to reduce your likely capital commitment.

Without that commitment, the project and the development of the first prototypes will cost three times your average annual after-tax profit for the past five years – roughly a quarter of your total net corporate worth. Even with it, the investment is huge.

Do you go for it?

If the year was 1952 and you were one of the Board members of Boeing, you'd say "Yes".

You'd decide to commission a project that will build the first large jet aircraft for the commercial market.

You'd decide to call it the Boeing 707.

You'd manage to persuade your major existing client, the US military, for which you have been building B-17 Flying Fortresses and the B-52 jet bomber, to buy a version of the new plane. It will use it as a fuelling plane and so reduce your gamble to $15 million.

Your main competitor Douglas Aircraft (later to become McDonnell-Douglas) would decide to carry on focusing on piston propeller planes for the commercial sector. It wouldn't be until 1958 that it would enter the now booming sector with the DC-8, letting you build an unsurpassable lead.

You'd go from building great bombers to being the leader in the new commercial jet market.

Your decision would change the face of the flying industry.

And the moral is that sometimes you have to take a leap of faith. What plans do you have that scare you?

65 THE T-SHIRT, THE FAIRY AND THE BRAND GUARDIAN

Roy Disney, a long-time senior executive and nephew of founder Walt Disney, never liked the idea of the Disney "brand". He once said, "Branding is for cattle." When asked, he would always stress the importance of creating stories and the products that these generated. Despite what he said, on numerous occasions, he was to play the key role as a guardian of the brand, ensuring it stayed true to its vision and core beliefs.

One of the many instances came in 2000. Times were tough and in particular the Consumer Products division was suffering; sales had fallen from $900 million in 1997 to just $386 million in 2000. Former Nike executive Andy Mooney was hired to try to rejuvenate the business.

Mooney's ideas were radical – at times very radical.

It was his idea to introduce a range of "vintage" t-shirts in upscale clothing shops like Fred Segal, Barneys and Hot Topic. The images on the shirts were taken from the archives. The issue wasn't the images but the way they were used.

One t-shirt showed Snow White, with a caption underneath

saying, "Hangs out with seven small men". Another showed Tinker Bell in a shot that made it look like she was eyeing up her own bottom in a mirror.

Roy wasn't happy and sent Mooney a handwritten note, which said: "You are positioning Tinker Bell as a prostitute."

For a brand dedicated to "the wonderful world of family entertainment", this was a step too far. Roy would never have used the words but what he was saying was, "Stop it, you're way off-brand".

Not surprisingly, the t-shirts were quickly withdrawn and Mooney was forced to apologize.

And the moral is that the brand needs to be able to say "No". What are the limits of what you would and wouldn't do with your brand?

66 A DRAMA AND A CRISIS

On 29 September 1982, 12-year-old Mary Kellerman woke up feeling sick. She was given one Extra Strength Tylenol capsule and, tragically, she died a few hours later. That same morning, postal worker Adam Janus took Tylenol and he too died shortly thereafter. To cope with their grief, Adam's brother, Stanley, and sister-in-law, Theresa, ingested Tylenol from Adam's bathroom, both dying within 48 hours.

Around the same time, tampered Tylenol would claim the lives of Mary Reiner, Paula Prince and Mary McFarland, bringing the total death toll to seven innocent Chicagoans.

An immediate investigation was launched. Having heard numerous radio reports detailing the incidents, two fire-fighters called in to report what they thought might be a possible connection between the deaths and Tylenol.

On testing, each of the capsules proved to be laced with potassium cyanide (KCN, which is an odourless, colourless substance that looks much like regular granulated salt). Each capsule contained KCN at a level toxic enough to provide thousands of fatal doses.

However, the fatal pills came from different production plants and were sold in different drug stores around the Chicago area. The police's conclusion was that someone was most likely tampering with the drug on the store shelves.

Johnson & Johnson found itself in a very difficult position. One of its leading products had killed seven people in a single city.

At that stage of its history, the company had never established a permanent public relations division or crisis management unit. With the help of the police and the FDA, however, Johnson & Johnson made a number of key decisions and took some decisive actions which still stand as examples of best practice.

On 5 October 1982, seven days after the first reported

death, Johnson & Johnson issued a nationwide recall of all Tylenol Extra Strength capsules. The nationwide recall was a brave and expensive decision, meaning that the company withdrew over 31 million bottles at an estimated retail value of over $100 million. It was the largest ever recall in the drugs industry. Johnson & Johnson's market share collapsed almost overnight from 35% to 8%. Customers were able to exchange Tylenol capsules for caplets, which were more difficult to tamper with.

As soon as the link to Tynlenol was established, Johnson & Johnson then set up two free 1-800 hotlines to deal with the massive panic and media interest. One was set up for the general public, answering questions and fielding the concerns of Tylenol users. The other was for news organizations, and used a daily pre-recorded message with updated statements from the company. Instead of trying to avoid publicity, CEO James Burke spoke directly to national news magazines and talk shows, giving the public a human face behind the business.

The company worked closely with the Chicago Police Department, FBI and FDA to identify suspects, and offered a $100,000 reward for information (though the Tylenol Murderer has never been found and the reward remains unclaimed).

Finally, company President Joseph Chiesa brought in new product consultant Martin Calle to work with him on the development of the world's first tamper-proof gelatine-enrobed capsule, called Tylenol Gelcaps.

On 11 November 1982, Tylenol was reintroduced with a new, triple-sealed package backing this with heavyweight advertising campaigns and price promotions where people could save up to $2.50 per bottle.

The campaigns positioned Tylenol as a brand you could trust.

To back this up, Johnson & Johnson continued to make improvements in quality control. Along with the new tamper-resistant packaging, it introduced random inspection procedures before the shipment of Tylenol to retailers.

In less than a year, Johnson & Johnson's market share had climbed back up to 29%, and within several years, Tylenol had once again become the most popular over-the-counter analgesic in the US. Today, it still holds a share of around 35%.

And the moral is that in the face of a crisis, brands should aim to over-compensate, not over-promise or ignore the problem. Do you know what you would do if a crisis struck your brand?

67 HAVEN'T I SEEN YOU SOMEWHERE BEFORE?

"Haven't I seen you somewhere before?" must be one of the oldest and corniest lines that air stewardesses have to put up with, but SAS air hostess Gia Bremberg put up with it more regularly than any of her colleagues ever did.

It might have been because she fitted the stereotypical

image of a Swedish woman; Gia was slim, tall, attractive with long, golden blonde hair, which when loose fell past her shoulders and almost to her waist.

However, the real reason was that lots of the men who asked her the question had indeed seen her before. Gia was the original blonde who washed her hair in a bucket by a well for the Timotei shampoo adverts, shown around the world between 1982 and 1991.

Gia was an 18-year-old schoolgirl when she answered an advert in her local Stockholm paper and won the job that changed her life. Unlike many models in other ads, Gia was a regular user of the brand:

"I've never dyed my hair and have only ever used shampoo and conditioner, then left it to dry naturally. And yes, it was always Timotei back then – I still remember its smell, like freshly-cut grass," she said when interviewed years later.

She was embarrassed if the ad came on when others were around: *"I never knew where to look. But my mum was always really proud."*

The money was good and helped Gia to buy her first apartment in Stockholm, but it was never enough to let her quit her full-time job. So she saved her annual holiday leave to film the ads.

One man who didn't use the "Haven't I seen you somewhere before?" line was her husband Mattias. He didn't recognize her, so Gia chose not to mention her role as the Timotei girl at first.

"He was really shocked when I told him about appearing in the ads. My hair was far shorter by then, so he never would have guessed. He remembered the [girl in the] *adverts well, but of course never imagined he'd end up marrying her."*

And the moral is that it pays to keep your feet on the ground (metaphorically that is). What's your plan B?

68 FRISKY AND PLAYFUL

In 1959, a reader sent a letter off to his favourite magazine. But instead of writing an address he drew a picture of a rabbit wearing a bow-tie on the envelope. The letter was duly delivered to the *Playboy* offices.

Things had obviously come a long way in the six years since Hugh Hefner launched his new magazine.

The title for the magazine was supposed to be *Stag Party*, but an unrelated outdoor magazine, *Stag*, contacted Hefner and informed him that it would legally protect its trademark and take him to court if he were to launch his magazine with that name.

Hefner, his wife Millie and co-founder and Executive Vice President Eldon Sellers met to discuss the problem and to seek a new name. Amongst other names they considered were Top Hat, Gentleman, Sir, Satyr, Pan and Bachelor, before Sellers suggested Playboy. Sellers' mother had worked for a short-lived firm called Playboy Automobile Company in Chicago, and on remembering it, Sellers thought it might be a good alternative.

It was an immediate sensation; it sold out all of its 50,000 circulation within a matter of weeks,[12] which despite his confidence must have delighted Hefner. He had been so worried, in fact, that the original issue did not carry a date, as he was unsure if or when there would be a second issue.

After this initial success, the next challenge was to create a brand identity. While the most obvious solution would have been to develop a stylish image of a "playboy", Hefner and his team realized that there were already two other magazines on the newsstands that used men as their icons – *Esquire* and *The New Yorker*. So rather than face another threat of a lawsuit, Hefner decided something different was needed.

"I selected a rabbit as the symbol for the magazine because of the humorous sexual connotation, and because he offered an image that was frisky and playful. I put him in a tuxedo to add the idea of sophistication.

"There was another editorial consideration, too. Since both The New Yorker *and* Esquire *use men as their symbols, I felt the rabbit would be distinctive; and the notion of a rabbit dressed up in formal evening attire struck me as charming, amusing...and right."*

The actual logo, depicting the stylized profile of a rabbit wearing a tuxedo bow tie, was created by art designer

[12] The cover price of that original issue was 50c. Copies of it in mint to near-mint condition sold for over $5,000 in 2002.

Art Paul who said some years later: "If I had any idea how important that little rabbit was going to be, I probably would have redrawn him a dozen times to make certain I was doing him justice, and I suppose none of those versions would have turned out as well as the original. As it was, I did one drawing and that was it. I probably spent all of half an hour on it."

And the moral is that great icons are distinctive and characterful. Does your brand have and harness a great icon?

69 FROM BLOODY AWFUL TO BLOODY AWESOME

The British Airways Board was established in 1971 to control two nationalized airline corporations – BOAC and BEA – and two smaller, regional airlines, Cambrian Airways and Northeast Airlines. On 31 March 1974, all four companies were merged to form British Airways.

Now fully and directly under government ownership, it was far from plain sailing for the business. Over the next decade, British Airways slid into a position where it was seen as an increasingly archaic public institution with a huge, unproductive work force and lax management that was producing huge losses.

A standing joke of the time was: "What does BA really stand for?", with the answer "Bloody Awful!"

The government dreamed of denationalizing the firm, and

turned to John King for their salvation, then Chairman of engineering firm Babcock International.

King's first major task was perhaps his most unpleasant one. Within a few months he reduced BA's bloated work force from 59,000 to 36,000, though to ease the impact, generous severance packages were offered to all who left voluntarily. The money for which was found by selling off surplus aircraft and some real estate holdings in the London area.

King then fired two long-standing agencies: the insurance agency that had handled BA's business for 60 years and the advertising agency Foote Cone & Belding who had been BA's agency for 36 years. He gave the account to the British-based agency Saatchi & Saatchi.

Next in line for a shake-up was the airline's Board. King's view was that the then current board was a largely ineffective bunch. It included an economist, a union leader, the head of another nationalized industry and a former treasury official. King transformed the Board with some top level professional appointments including a former Chairman of Barclays Bank International, a Director of Cadbury Schweppes and a bit later the Chairman of Unilever.

However, that still left the new Chief Executive role. King was determined not to hire an airline expert. "We were looking for someone who understood service," he said, "but there seemed to be an advantage in not knowing too much about the business. In my ignorance, I could do things I might not have done if I had been better informed." He wanted the same for his new CEO.

Finally in early 1983 Colin Marshall, then Deputy Chief Executive of Sears Holdings, was appointed.

"Morale really was appalling," he says now. "People had seen thousands of their colleagues go out the door, and they had no idea what would happen next. They needed some inspiration." So, Marshall set about moving from BA to BA, or in his words, "from Bloody Awful to Bloody Awesome".

New uniforms were designed for ticket agents, ground personnel, flight crews and even baggage handlers – the first change of garb in 20 years for male staff.

He repainted the fleet with distinctive new stripes and a company coat of arms bearing the motto "To Fly, To Serve".

But he understood that the motto wouldn't really mean anything unless the culture changed too, so all employees were made to attend a two-day seminar called "Putting People First". The workshops put British Airways employees in the customers' shoes. Flight attendants, for example, were asked to recall their own experiences in restaurants when meals were dumped unceremoniously in front of them.

Another strand to achieving the desired levels of service was meticulous attention to detail. Market research had shown that passengers responded much more positively when addressed by name. "Have a good flight, Mr. Lury", and when ticket agents made a point of using names, customer satisfaction scores rose about 60%. So this too became part of the training.

Next was an upgrade for BA's business-class service, which

included refurbishing lounges at major airports, putting seats with adjustable headrests in business-class cabins on most planes, and improving the quality of food. Renamed Club World, it was then advertised more widely.

At London's Heathrow airport special "hunters" were introduced; trouble-shooters who spoke a plethora of languages and roamed the terminal looking for confused passengers in need of assistance.

Timetables were reviewed, and unlike pre-Marshall days, when the airline's convenience could take precedence over the customer's, planes were by and large scheduled to take off when passengers wanted them to (leaving earlier or later for instance).

King's, Marshall's and the now reinvigorated employees' efforts paid off: the airline's financial results and reputation were transformed, and when in the advertising BA claimed to be "The World's Favourite Airline", it was no joke. In fact in 1987 when the Government denationalized it, the public offering of the British Airways stock was vastly oversubscribed.

As Colin Marshall probably said, "Bloody Awesome!"[13]

And the moral is that change is difficult but not impossible. What are the key actions you would make alongside any avowed intention to change?

[13] Unfortunately for BA, a combination of some complacency and the radical shifts in the industry (especially the emergence of low-cost airlines) meant the brand didn't live happily ever after and has in 2010 gone through a process not dissimilar to the transformation King and Marshall led. Interestingly one aspect of this re-launch has been a return and re-focusing on "To fly, to serve".

70 THIS LITTLE PIGGY WENT TO MARKET AND FOUND INSPIRATION

A litter of hungry pigs pushing and shoving, trying to get fed, seems an unlikely source of inspiration. But according to William Sitwell, author of *A History of Food in 100 Recipes*, it gave Clarence Saunders an idea.

It was in fact the basis for one of the most important innovations in modern retailing: the modern supermarket. In 1916, Clarence was on a train travelling from Indiana. The train slowed down at one point while passing a pig farm.

From his window, Clarence saw a large number of piglets gathering round their mother sow, all trying to get fed. It made him think of a strong similarity with the grocery stores he knew. In busy times there were never enough clerks, so that people would crowd around the counter trying to get served. He thought that there must be a better way of doing things – and had an idea.

Within a few months, Clarence Saunders opened his first store; a store with no counter and no staff to take orders. Instead, customers served themselves from the shelves and paid on the way out. Self-service and the supermarket had been born and was an immediate success.

Fast-forward seven years and there were 1,268 stores in his

chain, which he had named Piggly Wiggly in honour of his source of inspiration.[14]

And the moral is that great marketers are on duty 24 hours a day and are constantly curious. What have you seen in the last 24 hours which could inspire you?

71 IN HOT PURSUIT OF AN ICE-COLD TREAT (PART 1 OF 2)

Leo Stefanos was born in Greece but moved to Chicago's South Side where he opened a candy store. He named it Dove, which he chose for its "peaceful" quality. However, with three children, Michael, Chris and Amy, his life was often far from peaceful.

So perhaps it was no surprise that one day in 1956 the peace was shattered yet again. Michael, on spying an ice-cream truck going down the road outside the Stefanos' house, threw open the door and went haring down the street in hot pursuit of an ice-cold treat.

Leo was horrified and worried for the safety of his children, so decided to do something about it. His solution was to make his own ice-cream, one that would be good enough to keep Michael, Chris and Amy in the safety of their own home.

Leo took months to refine the recipe and finally settled on an extra thick slice of a block of creamy vanilla ice-cream dipped

[14] Unfortunately after a fantastic start, disaster struck, and a combination of financial mismanagement and poor stock trading saw Clarence go bankrupt and the business fail. Clarence lost everything, including a house complete with pig-pink rendering.

into premium thick chocolate which he named the Dove Bar. It was an instant success not just with Leo's children but all across Chicago; by the late 1970s over 1 million Dove Bars were being made every year.

In 1984 Mike Stefanos, who had taken over the business in 1977 when Leo passed away, presented the Dove Bar at the Fancy Food Show in Washington, DC and orders started coming in from around the country.

This increased popularity caught the eye of Mars and in 1986 they acquired the Dove brand.

And the moral of this story is that it's not only charity that begins at home. Can you use your family as your first (and maybe your fiercest) focus group?

72 STOLEN WITH PRIDE (PART 2 OF 2)

Magnum is an ice-cream brand owned by Unilever and sold under their Heartbrand line of products in many countries. It is a thick bar of vanilla ice cream, a little like a slice off a block of creamy ice-cream on a stick, covered in either white or dark chocolate.

The original Magnums, later rebranded as Magnum Classic, were sold in Europe in 1987. The true origins may be different but the story I have been told on many occasions is that the idea was "stolen with pride".

It starts with a Unilever ice-cream executive who went on holiday with his family to Chicago. Once there the weather was lovely and he and his family discovered and enjoyed a local favourite, the Dove Bar.

On the flight home it struck him that there was nothing like the delicious Dove Bars in the Unilever portfolio and indeed there was nothing like it in any of its competitors' portfolios in Europe.

Back at the office he re-created the experience he and his family so enjoyed and his team were immediately impressed.

Now they just needed a brand name and pretty soon "Magnum" was chosen, a name that worked on many levels. Literally, a magnum is "a large container of quality and taste", it has very positive conceptual associations of quality, something extra, quantity, of celebration (champagne) and it is phonetically suggestive too – magnificent, magic, yum, fun.

And the moral of this story is that it's ok to steal with pride. Are there ideas from other places in the world that could benefit your business?

73 A MEAL SO GOOD THEY BOUGHT THE RESTAURANT

Fernando Duarte was old friends with Robert Brozin, so when one day Fernando suggested that Robert come with him to a restaurant Fernando had recently discovered,

Robert was happy to oblige. When Fernando told him it was selling "the best chicken you'll ever eat", Robert knew it should be good, but little did he know how good it would be for him and indeed for their future.

The restaurant was in a small unassuming wooden building situated on the corner of the main road in Rosettenville, an old mining suburb in southern Johannesburg. It was called "Chickenland". Its speciality was piri piri chicken, a recipe that could trace its roots back through Portugal and Mozambique before arriving in South Africa.

History tells of how Portuguese settlers arrived in Mozambique in the 16th Century, where they quickly discovered the "pili pili" chili which was widely being used by the local population. Enjoying the kick it gave their food, the settlers began to use what they now called piri piri in their own daily cooking. They created a barbecue-style marinade sauce, among other recipes, and this became a favourite throughout Mozambique.

When the Witwatersrand gold rush of 1886 began, many Mozambicans of Portuguese origin went off in search of their fortunes, ultimately relocating to the areas around what was to become Johannesburg. Naturally they took their favourite foods, including piri piri chicken, with them.

Soon restaurants sprung up in these mining towns to feed the new and indeed the local population. One such restaurant was Chickenland, which had its own special recipe for piri piri chicken. It was this special recipe that the two friends, Fernando and Robert, enjoyed that evening in 1987. The meal was good; just as good as Fernando had promised it would be. So together the friends hatched a plan.

They decided to buy not just the recipe, but the restaurant too. Once the deal was done, they decided to re-name the restaurant "Fernando's" in honour of Durante's discovery, but quickly found out that there was already a restaurant by that name. They had to rename it. They chose "Nando's", an affectionate shortened version of Fernando.

For their new restaurant's look and feel the partners decided to incorporate influences from both Portugal and South Africa. The logo was derived from the Rooster of Barcelos from Portugal and the décor in that first, and all subsequent restaurants, includes original works of art done by South African artists.

Like those original Portuguese settlers, Nando's has gone travelling and "come home to roost" in more than 20 countries.

And the moral is that good brands often start with good products or services. Just how good are your products/ services?

74 APPEARANCES CAN BE DECEPTIVE

Having served his country in World War II, Darwin Eatna Smith returned to the United States, quietly determined to make something of himself. He put himself through night school at Indiana University but had to work the day shift at International Harvester to help pay his fees. During one shift, there was an accident and he lost a finger. Smith made little or no fuss: he still went to class that evening and, indeed, returned to work the very next day.

In 1958 he joined Kimberly-Clark's legal department and was named General Attorney one year later. He joined the Board of Directors in 1967, and took over as Chairman of the Board and Chief Executive Officer in 1971.

By the time he retired 20 years later, Kimberley-Clark had been transformed into the leading consumer paper products company in the world. Over his tenure, it delivered cumulative stock returns that were more than four times greater than those of the general market: better than Hewlett-Packard, 3M, Coca-Cola and General Electric, to name a few.

Along the way, he made a number of tough decisions, as when he concluded that the company's historical core business of coated paper had become too commoditized. Its economics were poor. Smith reasoned that the way forward was to put much greater emphasis on branded consumer goods, trading off more competition against higher margins.

To fund the new strategy, Smith announced the unthinkable: Kimberly-Clark would sell its mills, even its namesake in Kimberly, Wisconsin. The proceeds went into the fledgling consumer business, invested in brands such as Kleenex. At the same time, Smith pushed the company into new brands, one of which was a disposable diaper brand renamed Huggies.

So you might expect Smith to fit the stereotype of a successful CEO: a dynamic, big personality like Lee Iacocca or Jack

Welch. But Darwin Smith wasn't like that at all. He was shy, socially awkward and mild-mannered.

In one of the few interviews he gave, a journalist asked him to describe his management style. Dressed as ever in his very ordinary and plain J.C. Penney suit, Smith paused for consideration, before at last replying, "Eccentric".

In retirement, Smith summed up the approach responsible for his exceptional performance: "I never stopped trying to become qualified for the job."

And the moral is that appearances can be deceptive. Are you guilty of basing your truths on a surface trawl of your brand, category or consumer?

75 DON'T MINCE YOUR WORDS

Some years ago cattle farmers in Queensland, Australia were becoming worried at the falling sales of their beef. They decided that the answer might lie in an advertising campaign.

They duly invited a number of advertising agencies from Sydney to come up and pitch for the business, but the slick planners and creative types didn't mix well with the straight-talking ranchers. The ranchers didn't think much of all their talk of brand positionings, core target groups and image building, and didn't see the need to differentiate between stimulus and response.

In short, they thought the "luvvies" were talking a load of bullshit. The admen didn't seem to get the fact that the ranchers just wanted to sell more beef. So the creatives and the suits went back to Sydney empty-handed. The farmers were still convinced that they needed something simple, strong and direct, however. Since it didn't seem that difficult, they decided they would do the ads for themselves.

"What's so difficult about it? All we want to do is tell the bastards to eat more beef," said one.

And so one of the world's most famous campaigns was born – on billboards, T-shirts, in butchers' windows and on car stickers, the (in)famous tagline was soon appearing:

"Eat More Beef You Bastards".

And the moral is that it pays to know your target audience. With what tone of voice should you be talking to your potential customers?

76 THE APRIL FOOL

Despite the fact that the company was founded on 1 April, William Wrigley Jr was to prove that he was no fool.

29-year-old William had moved to Chicago from Philadelphia in 1891 with $32 to his name and the idea of putting that name to a business selling "Wrigley's Scouring Soap". He quickly decided to offer incentives to encourage people to buy his soap, and one incentive he used was baking powder. The incentive proved to be so popular that he switched to selling baking powder. Keeping his policy of incentivizing sales, he began offering two packages of chewing gum for each purchase of a can of baking powder.

Yet again William found that there seemed to more interest in his incentive than in his core product, and so he changed direction again and began to produce chewing gum.

One of his first aims was to challenge the stereotype that only women should chew gum. Two of the company's earliest products – Sweet Sixteen Orange and Lotta Gum – revolutionized chewing gum's appeal, spreading interest to the youth market and then to the public at large.

In another act of what could have been foolishness, he decided during the economic depression of 1893 that he would introduce two new flagship products: Wrigley's Spearmint and Juicy Fruit. Yet again he proved the sceptics wrong and the brands were an immediate success.[15]

So when an even more debilitating economic downturn arrived in 1907, Wrigley did another foolish thing and mortgaged just about everything he owned to launch a massive advertising campaign. Surprise, surprise – it was another success.

And the moral is that some see opportunities where others only see risk. What foolish thing should you be doing?

[15] In another move that many at the time might have seen as foolish, Wrigley Jr established himself as one of the nation's leading champions of employee rights and benefits, creating a health and welfare department in Wrigley's Chicago factory in 1916 and granting his employees both Saturdays and Sundays off in 1924. During the Great Depression, the company went one step further, boldly setting minimum wage levels so its workers could have financial security during one of the nation's darkest hours.

THE MORALS

THE PRISONER AND THE PENGUIN (Penguin)
A recognizable brand icon is a powerful communication equity. What communication equity does your brand own?

THE TATTOOED ANKLE (Nike)
Great brands inspire great loyalty. How will your brand inspire this level of loyalty?

FROM SWITZERLAND WITH LOVE (Barbie)
Old ideas can be reinterpreted for new markets. What ideas from other markets could you use to deliver innovation in your own market?

THE MOUSE AND THE CAR PARK ATTENDANT (Disney)
Everyone in service brands is in marketing. Are your employees delivering your brand in their interactions with the public?

THE SAMPLE OF ONE (Virgin Atlantic)
Sometimes you don't need great swathes of market research. Is all your market research really necessary?

THE CHOCOLATE LOVER TAKEN FOR A FOOL (Gü)
Brand naming is never easy. Do you know what you want from any new brand names?

BEAUTY AND THE TWO UNDERTAKERS (The Body Shop)
PR is not only one of the most powerful media for a brand, but it's also free. What is it about your brand that would make a PR story?

THE CHARM BRACELET AND THE 52 FUNDAMENTAL ERRORS (Monopoly)
Don't be too proud to admit your mistakes. How can you change a past mistake into a future opportunity?

TO DYE FOR (Clairol)
Sometimes, creating a truly powerful brand or campaign means changing the way people think. Should your brand challenge a convention?

THE INSPIRATIONAL BIRTHDAY CAKE (Viennetta)
Inspiration for innovation can come from adjacent markets. Where are you looking for your next innovation?

THE MANAGEMENT WHO FIRED THEMSELVES (Intel)
Good enough is not enough. What are you planning to do that is groundbreaking not just good enough?

WHEN 250,000 PEOPLE WERE WRONG (Coca-Cola)
You need to take extra care when adapting classic brands. What are the negotiable and non-negotiable elements of your brand?

THE NOISY ENGINE AND THE QUIET CLOCK (Rolls Royce and Ogilvy & Mather)
It pays to interrogate your product until it squeaks. What is your product's true competitive advantage?

THE PARTY WITH EXTRA TOYS (Ann Summers)
If your customers won't come to you, go to your customers. What new channels could you use to connect with your customers?

THE AD THAT DIDN'T LIE (Volkswagen and Doyle Dane Bernbach)
A great ad is often a truth well told. What truth should you be telling about your brand?

A MODEL BRAND, A MODEL BRAND MANAGER (Kelly Brook)
Every brand needs a passionate brand manager. Are the people working on your brand really committed to it?

A LITTLE WEIRDNESS GOES A LONG WAY (Nike and Wieden +Kennedy)
Sometimes inspiration strikes when you least expect it. What could you do to take your mind off a problem and let your mind wander?

THE AGENCY THAT SAID "NO" (HHCL and Martini)
A principle isn't a principle until it costs you money (but in the long run, remember that it will probably make you money). What are the principles to which your brand will stay true, even when tempted to do otherwise?

THE HAMBURGERS THAT DIDN'T GET BURNT (McDonald's)
A brand is a unit of social currency and should play a role in the wider community. What does your brand contribute to the local or wider community in which it exists?

THE JEALOUS FRENCHMAN (Mouton Cadet)
Brands are a guarantee of quality. How closely do you monitor and control your product or service?

THE GOLDEN WEB (Goldcorp)
A fresh pair of eyes can bring a fresh perspective, 1,000 fresh pairs eyes can open your eyes to lots of new opportunities. What problem could you outsource?

FLIPPING THE HARP (Guinness and the Irish Government)
Creating and managing your identity is a key responsibility for any management team. Are all the key elements of your identity protected?

THE POWER OF TWO LITTLE WORDS (Ratners)
If you don't believe in your brand, why should anyone else? Are you and your fellow employees true advocates for your brand?

THE STARS' FREE GIFTS (Trivial Pursuit)
Word of mouth is the best form of advertising. What could you do to generate positive word of mouth?

THE PLASTIC PEOPLE WITH THE PLASTIC SMILES (Oxo)
Advertising doesn't need to be glossy to be successful, empathy is a powerful tool. How well do you really know the motivations and realities of your customers?

BATMAN AND THE BALL BOYS (*Batman*)
Sometimes you can out-think rather than just out-spend your competition. Instead of wishing for a bigger budget, ask yourself what would you do if your advertising and promotion spend was to be cut in half?

THE TIGER AND THE COMMITTEE (Disney Animal Kingdom)
Even the most hardened professional is a human, and the use of theatre can be a powerful decision-making tool. How can you dramatize your next presentation?

SOME BINS AND SOME FRUIT (innocent)
Market research doesn't need to be complicated to be useful. Could you simplify or reduce the amount of research you do and still get the information you truly need?

IT TAKES ALL SORTS (Bassett's Liquorice Allsorts)
Serendipity can be a source of innovation. Does your innovation process allow for chance and the wild card?

THE STITCHING AND THE EMAIL (Nike)

Social media opens out a world of possibilities – but these aren't always positive. Have you thought through all the implications of your social media strategy?

THE SPELLING MISTAKE, THE BACKRUB AND 100 ZEROS (Google)

Not all mistakes produce bad results. Looking back over mistakes you may have made in the past, how can you capitalize on something that went wrong?

THE LIPSTICK AND THE AIRLINE (Henkel Pritt Stick)

Inspiration can strike at anytime, anywhere. Are you constantly curious, always attuned looking for new ideas?

THE BANK THAT LIKES TO SAY NO (ING Direct)

It can pay to zig when the world zags. Is there an opportunity in the opposite of what all your competitors are doing?

BROTHERLY LOVE? (Adidas and Puma)

Competition is often good for both parties. How can you use your competition to your advantage?

THE WOMAN OF MANY FACES (Betty Crocker)

People like people, making personification a powerful branding tool. How can you give your brand a human face?

MORE THAN A PROMISE (Avis)

A brand is more than a promise, it's a responsibility. Are you making sure you live up to your responsibilities?

THE INCISIVE LETTER K (Kodak)

Creativity thrives on a tight brief. Do you make sure every creative brief you write has clear and tight guidelines to guide the thinking and help your assessment of the work?

THE MEERKATS, THE COMPETITION AND A HEALTHY DOSE OF NECESSITY (comparethemarket.com)

You don't have to be first to market to succeed. What do you need to do to make a late entry into the market distinctive and compelling?

DADDY'S GOOD LUCK CHARM (Coca-Cola)

Great brands make emotional as well as functional connections. What emotion does your brand evoke?

M IS FOR MOM'S NIGHT OFF (McDonald's)

People react to messaging both rationally and emotionally, on a conscious and subconscious level. What are people really taking out from your communications?

GOOD LUCK'S BAD LUCK (Good Luck)

Celebrity-based advertising affects both the celebrity and the brand. If you use a celebrity, will they add value both to your proposition and to their own?

10 (Tesco)

A clearly defined vision and set of values should be at the core of your brand. Are yours clearly defined and known throughout the organization?

NO FRILLS BUT LOTS OF LAUGHS (Southwest Airlines)

A little humour can go a long way. What are you doing that will put a smile on your customers' faces?

THE NO SCOLD GUARANTEE (Honda)

Early prototyping can identify early problems. How soon in your innovation process do you develop real prototypes?

THE LONELY SMOKER (Strand)

What people hear isn't always what you say. What are people really hearing when you speak to them?

THE LITTLE CAR'S CONTRIBUTION TO LOW-COST FURNITURE (IKEA)

Necessity can be the mother of invention. Should you take a fresh look at some of the challenges facing you and your brand?

THE GLUE THAT WOULDN'T STICK (3M Post-it Notes)

Not all innovations start with a consumer insight. What technologies do you have which could offer new benefits for your customers?

THE 5,000 FAILURES (Dyson)

Sometimes it pays to think the unthinkable and do things "wrong" Could you do something better by doing it wrong?

THE BATS, THE PRINCE AND THE SICK NOTE (Barcardi)

A picture or indeed an icon can be worth more than words. Could you be making more of the images and icons linked to your brands?

THE DEAR JAMES LETTER (Lego)

Little gestures can have a big impact. What are the little gestures you could and perhaps should be making?

IF AT FIRST YOU DON'T SUCCEED, CHEW AND CHEW AGAIN (Hershey)

If at first you don't succeed, try and try again? Are you in danger of giving up on something too soon?

ANY COLOUR AS LONG AS IT IS ARMY GREEN (Volkswagen)

Sometimes from the ashes of disaster grow the roses of success. How can you use a past failure to drive future success?

A VERY SPECIAL BREW (Carlsberg Special Brew)

Products may need to be evolved or repositioned to find their most successful niche. Have all your products or services found their optimum position?

THE WHITE KNIGHT AND THE CHOC-ICE (Virgin Atlantic)

It pays to put yourself in your customers' shoes. When did you last "mystery shop" your own brand.

A TIRED OLD STORY? (Nordstrom)

Empowering employees can power your brand. Do you trust your staff to always do the right thing?

THE 13-TON WRISTWATCH (Swatch)

It pays to have solutions to future problems ready in advance. Are you really thinking ahead about the challenges you may face?

THE ROLLS ROYCE AND THE KETTLE (JCB)

Even when you think you have thought of everything, there is always room for improvement. What are you doing to make your offer even better?

RED STAR AT NIGHT, BREWERS DELIGHT? (Heineken)

A little magic, a little mystery can add to a brand's appeal. Where is the magic in your brand?

THE NO NEWS GOOD NEWS (London Transport)

Nothing bad happening can sometimes be as good as something good happening. What performances are you taking for granted?

FROM THE ISLE OF SKY TO BUCKINGHAM PALACE, A 171-YEAR JOURNEY (Drambuie)

Not all innovations are overnight successes. Are you keeping faith in ideas that you believe will be slow-burn successes?

WHERE'S EDDIE? (Eddie Stobart)

Your brand image and the impressions it makes are important. How do you ensure you always project the image you want?

THE PARSIMONIOUS BOSS AND THE $99 REQUISITIONS (3M)

Ideas aren't the only problem; executing them right is crucial too. Do you have a great idea that just needs more work?

THE INSANELY GREAT $50-MILLION GAMBLE (Pixar)

Your brand is like a bank account. When are you going to make the next deposit?

WOULD YOU, WOULDN'T YOU? (Boeing)

Sometimes you have to take a leap of faith. What plans do you have that scare you?

THE T-SHIRT, THE FAIRY AND THE BRAND GUARDIAN (Disney)

Brands need to be able to say "No". What are limits of what you would and wouldn't do with your brand?

A DRAMA AND A CRISIS (Tylenol)

In the face of a crisis, brands should aim to over-compensate not over-promise or ignore the problem. Do you know what you would do if a crisis struck your brand?

HAVEN'T I SEEN YOU SOMEWHERE BEFORE? (Timotei)

It pays to keep your feet on the ground. What's your plan B?

FRISKY AND PLAYFUL (*Playboy*)

Great icons are distinctive and characterful. Does your brand have and harness a great icon?

FROM BLOODY AWFUL TO BLOODY AWESOME (BA)

Change is difficult but not impossible. What are the key actions you would make alongside any avowed intention to change?

THIS LITTLE PIGGY WENT TO MARKET AND FOUND INSPIRATION (Piggly Wiggly)

Great marketers work 24 hours a day; they are constantly curious. What have you seen in the last 24 hours which could inspire you?

IN HOT PURSUIT OF AN ICE-COLD TREAT:(Part 1 of 2 – Dove)

It's not only charity that begins at home. Can you use your family as your first (and maybe your fiercest) focus group?

STOLEN WITH PRIDE: (Part 2 of 2 – Magnum)
It's ok to steal with pride. Are there ideas from other places in the world that could benefit your business?

A MEAL SO GOOD THEY BOUGHT THE RESTAURANT (Nando's)
Good brands often start with good products or services. Just how good are your products/services?

APPEARANCES CAN BE DECEPTIVE (Kimberley-Clark)
Appearances can be deceptive. Are you guilty of basing your truths on a surface trawl of your brand, category or consumer?

DON'T MINCE YOUR WORDS (Australian Beef)
It pays to know your target audience. With what tone of voice should you be talking to your potential customers?

THE APRIL FOOL (Wrigley)
Some see opportunities where others only see risk. What foolish thing should you be doing?

ABOUT THE AUTHOR

Giles Lury is a VW Beetle-driving, Lego watch-wearing, Disney-loving, Chelsea-supporting father of five who also happens to be Chairman of The Value Engineers and author of three previous marketing related books – *Brandwatching*, *Researchwatching* and *Adwatching* (all published by Blackhall Publishing, Dublin).

He has worked in advertising, market research, design and corporate identity but his (work-related) heart belongs to the brands that he has had the opportunity to work on, many of which are included in this book.

If you have enjoyed these stories or have a brand story to share, please do visit his blog www.theprisonerandthepenguin.com or contact him through giles.lury@thevalueengineers.com.

ABOUT THE VALUE ENGINEERS

The Value Engineers is a leading brand strategy consultancy that aims to help create value through brands and branding. It provides insight, brand development strategies and innovation that allow its clients to out-think, out-manoeuvre and out-perform their competition.

Those clients span both categories and geographies as The Value Engineers work across fmcg, service, corporate and b2b brands around the world from its two offices: one in the UK and one in the USA.

www.thevalueengineers.com